No Easy Road

REAL STORIES
FROM THE CENTRAL VALLEY

Table of Contents

DEDICATION

This book is dedicated to Steve and Randi Smart
and Rick and Debbie Berbereia.
Both couples have looked into the face of family tragedy
and have overcome. There is *No Easy Road*, but there are
those who continue to inspire and bring hope to all.

Acknowledgements

I would like to thank Dennis Sunderland for making this book a reality; Regan Sunderland, for the vision he had from the beginning and the effort he put into making this book come to life; and the people of Bethel Family Worship Center, for their boldness and vulnerability in sharing their real-life stories.

This book would not have been published without the amazing efforts of our Project Manager, Jeannette Scott. Her untiring resolve pushed this project forward and turned it into a stunning victory. Thank you for your great fortitude and diligence. I would also like to thank our invaluable Proofreader, Melody Davis, for all the focus and energy she has put into perfecting our words. Huge thanks to our Executive Editor, Nicole Phinney Lowell, and our Editor in Chief, Michelle Cuthrell.

Lastly, I want to extend our gratitude to Ann Clayton, our Graphic Artist, whose talent and vision continually astound us. We are so blessed to have you as a part of this team.

Daren Lindley
President and CEO
Good Catch Publishing

The book you are about to read
is a compilation of authentic life stories.
The facts are true, and the events are real.
These storytellers have dealt with crisis, tragedy, abuse
and neglect and have shared their most private moments,
mess-ups and hang-ups in order for others to learn and
grow from them. In order to protect the identities of those
involved in their pasts, the names and details of some
storytellers have been withheld or changed.

INTRODUCTION

Frustration. Guilt. Shame. Anxiety. Anger. Confusion.

These are just some of the words that express how people feel when they realize their lives are not what they expected. The journey of life can be full of mountaintop experiences: weddings, the birth of a child or a promotion. However, it isn't too long until we are faced with a crisis of some sort. We can find ourselves elated one minute and devastated the next. How do we hold on? Can we get back up? How do we cope? Will there be a rainbow at the end of my storm? One thing is for sure: There are *No Easy Roads*!

What you are about to read are the stories of seven individuals who, like you, are trying to navigate the roadmap of life. Their stories of hardship, broken promises, sickness, loss and abuse will not only captivate you but will inspire you to keep on keeping on. They have not only found the strength to overcome the obstacles that this life throws in their path but will reveal to you the secrets of their breakthroughs. May you enjoy the journey you are about to embark on!

"Strength does not come from winning. Your struggles develop your strengths. When you go through hardships and decide not to surrender, that is strength."
~Arnold Schwarzenegger

Soul of the Exile
The Story of Ramon
Written by Richard Drebert

"Don't talk to anyone, hijo."

"Si, Mama."

My mother threw a burrito into a plastic lunch pail and kissed my head before I trotted down the road to the bus stop.

The bus was very full today. I paid the driver and scooted against a window, ignored by street vendors with crates of noisy chickens, an old man with a pig on his lap, fruit pickers and women wrestling hijos (children). After about 30 minutes, the bus downshifted to a stop near the Mexico border station, and a few of us spilled out. My eyes darted everywhere. Wary. Noticing everything.

The sun glared off lines of idling cars and semi-trucks as they waited to be inspected or waved through the border station into the Promised Land. I beat a path in the opposite direction, a route that I followed every day. Not even the richest nation on earth could plug every hole in its vast border — and I knew more than one tear in the border fence where a skinny 6 year old could shinny through.

Mama had assigned me an important daily task: to carry lunch to my stepdad, who worked over the border, inside the United States of America. After completing my mission, I would work for a while, carrying boards or pulling nails with my stepfather. Afterward, I would skitter across the fence, back to the bus stop and home where Mama waited on pins and needles for me. She would ask about Papa, and I would tell her all the details of my day while she cooked tortillas and beans.

My 3-year-old brother, Chico, toddled around the dirt floor, and Mama would wash him before the three of us crawled into our single bed in the corner of our small hut. I usually couldn't sleep for a long time. In my mind, I *lived* every moment of the following day. My family depended on me.

But today after delivering his lunch, Papa let me go late. I worried about missing the bus that would carry me back home, but it did no good to argue, especially if my stepdad was drinking. Now, I raced along the desert landscape like a jackrabbit, while the blazing sun glowed against the mountain range. I loped along the American side of the border toward my favorite gap in the fence when I heard the dogs.

Every fruit picker or domestic who crosses the border illegally fears the short-haired black and tan demon dogs. No one can outrun them, and I felt a twinge of terror as I cast a glance over my shoulder.

They were coming. My fingers clawed into the chain-link fence. I had to cross *now.* I could never reach my tear in the border before they chased me down. Strands of barbed wire coiled at the top of the 10-foot fence, and I struggled to straddle it without ripping my clothes. I slipped, then fell onto the barbs, trying to stifle a scream. It came out, anyway.

A deep slice ran red at a rip in my pants, and I gritted my teeth, clambering down to safe Mexican dirt. The authorities didn't care who lived or died on our Mexico side.

I ran a little way, listening to the dogs and their handlers from a safe distance, then sat teary-eyed beside a tall sage. I had to hurry. I tore a strip from my shirt and staunched the bleeding before limping my way south to the bus stop.

"Dios mio! Ramon! What happened to you?"

Mama cleaned out the deep cut in my flesh as I told my story, and she shuddered a little. I didn't fulfill my duty the next day, but as soon as I healed up, I carried Papa's pail again.

I crossed the fence illegally dozens of times until Papa set up my "free pass" to come and go through the border station. My stepdad had border agents as amigos. I learned to make friends with the intimidating men with guns and dark glasses, too.

I was about 7 when Mama decided it was time for all of us to live in the Promised Land. Papa was a U.S. citizen, and he didn't want us to come, but Mama set her heart on us being together as a family. She began saving her money to pay a coyote (a people smuggler).

࿇࿇࿇

My mother was born in the heavily forested Southwestern part of Mexico. Her earliest childhood memories include having a bloated belly from severe malnutrition. Mama lived in a primitive culture where out-of-wedlock pregnancy dishonored her heritage. Seeing Mama's swelled tummy under her blouse, my grandmother wrongly believed that she was carrying a child.

"B****! Whore! You shame your familia!"

The beatings at the hands of my grandmother changed Mama's life forever. Paralyzed from the waist down, my mother lay in a room by herself for weeks, immobile, infected with sores and insect bites.

"Get up! You have a baby coming. Get ready to take care of it!"

Her mother screamed at her every day, but Mama couldn't move.

In a society where newborn girls were scorned and boys treasured (for their ability to support the family), Mama lay moaning in the dark while scorpions crawled over her blankets.

It wasn't until a passerby looked through the pane-less window one morning and saw Mama's emaciated body that Grandma admitted her folly. Relatives loaded Mama into a cart and took her to a hospital in the city. It took a full year of healthy food and therapy before she healed enough to go home again.

While convalescing, Mama learned how to care for others, and her aptitude for learning a nurse's skills drew attention from physicians. She was offered an opportunity to take up nursing as a vocation, but my grandfather whisked her back to their poverty-ridden life. He said that she needed to learn to keep a home for a husband someday.

Her paralysis never completely left her limbs, and over the years she has suffered periods of sudden immobility. Doctors said that her injuries would prevent her from having children, but she prayed, "God, give me 20! I promise to take care of every one!"

What she endured as a child at the hands of those she loved echoed over and over throughout her life. At 14, Mama *did* have a child, conceived in a violent rape that happened while she stayed with trusted relatives. After the baby was born, her family abandoned them. Her first son, my brother, became ill and died in her arms.

Mama ran away to the city, where she apprenticed to a man with an adobe oven, and she learned to bake breads. By trading bread for labor, Mama drafted village children to haul clay from a riverbank to build her own oven inside a hut where she lived alone. In time, she added chickens to her inventory and sold poultry and eggs to local customers.

When her mother saw how successful she had become, she dropped off my mother's four brothers and sisters to be raised by her. At 15 years old, Mama's drive to succeed cast a bright light on her future. And although she believed herself to be the "ugly girl with a limp," a fisherman from the coast married her.

Mama had her second son, and named me Ramon, when she was just 16 years old. She continued to work, and my father spent weeks at sea, but he was home long enough to give me a baby brother, Chico. My family was upwardly mobile in our community, profiting from my mother's entrepreneurship and my father's paychecks from fishing. Out of jealousy, friends of my mother plotted to steal my father away by offering their daughters to the 45-year-old seafaring man. He gladly took them up on the offers.

Mama took him to task for unfaithfulness and growing neglect of Chico and me.

In a parting conversation with my mother, Papa said something like, "I was raised a loner. Let my sons be loners, too."

My father was an infant when his whole family had been slaughtered in a Mexican blood feud. His mother had wrapped him in a blanket and run to the forest to save him from the butchery. With no family ties except his elderly mother, Papa had run away to the sea. Sadly, the winds of bitterness filled his soul, and no one could set him on a new tack. Packing up his duffel, he boarded a ship and sank into an ocean of selfishness. I never saw him again.

After my father abandoned us, my mother made the mistake of leaving Chico and me with Grandma for a few months to take a job in another town as a restaurant cook. It would be the last time she would ever allow Grandma to be part of our lives.

A messenger found Mama at work one day. "If you

want to see your son Chico again, your mother says come quick."

Mama traveled several hours by bus to Grandma's house, kicking herself for being so desperate that she left Chico and me with the same woman who had abused her. But what choice did she have? A good job as a cook didn't come around that often in Mexico. She had no one to take care of her boys while she worked, and her mother had offered. Mama's survival instinct had trumped her good sense.

When she arrived at Grandma's little shack, Mama gasped when she saw me. I stood in a girl's dress, the prettiest nina anyone ever saw. She was speechless until she saw Chico inside the house. He lay in his own filth, covered in sores. Mama gathered us up and headed for the hospital, while Grandma screamed epithets after her.

Did her own mother hate her so much as to watch her grandson slowly die? And why would she dash me against a crisis of identity?

Chico recovered his physical strength over time, but the trauma set him back years in motor skills and ability to speak. I became his mentor, his defender. At our shack in the Mexican border town where my mother worked, he would sit in bed and rock for hours, and somehow I had the presence of mind to communicate with him. I knew what he needed and cherished him with a passionate, brotherly love. As I grew older, Mama relied upon me to help her care for Chico and later for my other siblings, too.

My stepdad, Fernando, entered our lives as a big happy fellow that my mother approved to help raise Chico and me. We moved into his little house together, and in about two years, Mama had two more sons: Manuel and Daniel.

He was from Texas, and this made him a celebrity in Mexican circles. He knew his way around the United States and took us across the border for visits to places like the beach and malls, just like an American family. What Mama didn't know was that Fernando had a mistress named Tequila.

Liquor twisted his mind to think like a dark, hateful demonio. Two obsessions haunted his mind when he was drunk: my mother, whom he incessantly accused of sleeping with other men, and his knives. He loved to throw his knives at trees or targets — and his woman.

"Fernando is coming home. He's got a bottle of Tequila, Ramon …"

I knew my job.

"Help me, Chico!" We grabbed up little Manuel and Daniel like flour sacks and stumbled out the door. We stayed as quiet as we could in a shed or in a field somewhere, listening for hours to Mama crying and pleading, until Fernando passed out.

At daylight Mama came looking for the four of us, and we went inside. Snores and man noises growled from the bedroom, and Mama ran water in the sink, dabbing a washrag on cuts or bruises, wherever my stepdad had concentrated his fists, slaps or knife blade.

Sometimes Mama called the police, who came and beat Fernando to a pulp, just to teach him not to cause a ruckus so they had to come. Mama had to nurse him then.

After a few years, Fernando eased out of our family for a short time, wandering to and from work on both sides of the border. Mama struggled, keeping food on the table by working in a restaurant, until a partial paralysis caught up with her. We moved into a plank shed with one bed, and Mama put in a little adobe oven to work baking bread.

"Do your best to get some money for each loaf. Okay?"

At first I came home dejected, breadless and almost centavo-less. Customers took advantage of a 6-year-old salesman.

"Don't worry. You'll get better. Try again tomorrow. Now let's count centavos and pesos again … I give you two pesos for a loaf, and you give me how much back?"

In time, no one cheated me. I handled my bread sales like a Mexican cash register.

అఠఠ

Our coyotes were here. They pulled into our designated parking lot, wearing identical sweat-ringed cowboy hats, coveralls and heavy black bigotes (mustaches). We hadn't seen Fernando in months, but heard tidbits of his whereabouts through mutual friends. Our coyotes knew our stepdad, and for a price "the twins" offered to take us across the border and deposit us at a safe house somewhere near where Fernando worked.

In a big station wagon, my three brothers, Mama and I joined a dozen other sweating brown men, women and children — our legs and arms squeezed tightly against our bodies to give others a little more room. A big armed Mexican hombre, with arms the size of pork shanks, leaned on the window and seemed to know one of the twins who handed him papers.

We all stared straight ahead like lifeless figurines until we cleared the border station. On the States side, Mama started breathing again, and people carried on conversations. The twins dropped us and our scant luggage at a house where a family of white people invited us into a room with a single bed.

This was the first time I felt the sting of bigotry in our new country. The white children who owned the house seemed to think that they were better than poor Mexican kids. I didn't care. I was in the United States! Mama and my brothers were with me, and we would see Fernando soon. Perhaps he wouldn't be drinking. He had citizenship and knew *everything* about the country!

We were sorely disappointed by Fernando's unenthusiastic welcome. We had invaded his country. The border had been a line that we never should have crossed. Mama got the message but said, "Just give him time. He needs to adjust to having his familia close, that's all."

In the meantime we got a ride to Fresno County, where my mother's auntie gave us a temporary home. Mom's legs had gained back their strength again, and she landed a job in the orchards picking oranges. We saw

Fernando once in a while when he spent the night with Mama, but it was me who stepped into the role as Papa when Mama worked 12-hour days. I babysat my brothers and sisters, and soon Mama added one more to my brood. Pretty little Christa came into our lives. And then there were *five* …

Olives, grapes, almonds, tomatoes, oranges. While Mama picked according to the seasons, we wore out our welcome at Auntie's house — and I couldn't wait to leave.

Auntie's 15-year-old dysfunctional son liked to babysit us sometimes when everyone was gone — at least babysitting was what *he* called it. I was exactly half his age when he molested me. It happened more than once, and I buried my helpless anger deep, to keep from causing trouble with his family that was trying to help us. It would have crushed my mother to know she had once again, out of desperation, left her loved ones in the care of a deviant.

Looking back, I see clearly that an evil force targeted me to wreck and reroute my masculine identity. Auntie's son dressed me up like a girl, just as my grandmother had.

❧❧❧

Illegal.

"If I don't come back, Ramon, you need to keep the family together. Don't let anyone separate you!"

When Mama left for work each day, I fought back a growing terror that she would be deported back to Mexico, and we would never see her again. My stepdad had connections to get Mama legal, but he refused to help.

"And don't open the door to anyone, understand?"

"Si, Mama."

"If you can't keep your little sister or brothers quiet, get everyone into the bathroom and stick towels against the bottom of the door. Then silencio!"

I held my 7-month-old sister, Christa, on my hip, and we waved to my mother as she left. She always left a stack of burritos in the refrigerator for us, but she never took a lunch herself. The fruit of the vine, tree or bush filled her belly. Whatever was in season, she consumed.

At home I discovered the same talent as she: creating something tasty out of whatever leftovers we had — whether in the kitchen or in life.

When the California Child Protective Services showed up at our door, Mama panicked. She enrolled us in school immediately; at the same time, we found out that her older sister needed a temporary home. Mama moved her into the apartment so that she could take care of Christa and the little ones.

At school, I was ahead of my class in math; in English, I was far behind — and so it went almost all the way through high school.

Mama had a first-grade education, but she had taught us to read English and Spanish before we ever attended our first class.

And while we were in school, Mama used every resource she could find to get ahead, for as long as she *might* remain in this remarkable land of opportunity. She taught us never to dwell on the possibility of deportation. She just worked and thought about today.

❧❧❧❧

In the ghetto, a shy little Mexican boy was ripe fruit to stomp on. I had been having problems with bullies in the neighborhood when I walked to school, and Mama absolutely forbid me to fight. My brothers and sisters had no room to play at our apartment complex, and Mama was growing more and more fearful for our safety.

One day, Fernando showed up, and Mama agreed to move to a migrant camp as a family. My stepdad refused to work in the orchards, but he had other opportunities, he said. We settled into a cottage, and us kids went wild with a huge yard to play in. One central restroom with showers and washroom sat in the middle of the shabby complex, to service workers and their families.

But it was a big mistake moving to the migrant camp with Fernando. He enjoyed snorting a new poison with his Tequila, *cocaine*, and it turned him into a monster.

Mama worked in the fields or orchards, and after hours she networked to start a new business venture. She met a dairyman and bought his milk to make cheese. She sold the cheese to the migrant workers in the camp, while my stepdad collected discarded electronics and wiring to strip out copper, aluminum and other metals. He sold the metals to salvage yards. I got my old babysitting job back instead of going to school.

When Fernando grabbed Mama and threw her on the cottage floor, Mama's eyes met mine, and she mouthed the words, *"Get them out ..."*

I gathered up my brothers and sisters, and Chico helped me herd them toward the bathrooms, watching over my shoulder as my stepdad flung Mama outside. Fernando's great open hands whapped Mama's face and head mercilessly until she lay still in the dirt, stunned. Fernando stopped to rest a moment, and a woman opened a door to the washroom, beckoning us children inside.

The last thing I saw before we shut the door was Mama lying like a dead woman. Soon her weeping filled the camp again, and the door to our cottage slammed shut. She was inside with Fernando. Cocaine kept the demons awake in my stepdad all night, and he kept beating Mama until daylight.

I recall someone shoving Doritos and hot sauce through the door in the morning, and no one wanted to confront the damage done inside our cottage. A woman who bought cheese from Mama fed us during the next day as we hid. The door to our cottage never opened, and the silence was worse to me than Mama's cries of pain.

The next day, the cottage door burst open, and Fernando's fingers tangled in Mama's dark hair as he drug her into the yard again. Police arrived before he killed her, and they cuffed Fernando, who was nearly incoherent.

"It's okay! The police are here, children," a woman said, and we ran to Mama who lay slumped on the steps of our cottage. She could barely speak to the policemen, and

Fernando stared malevolently at Mama as the cops drove him away. A demonic obsession clawed at Fernando's mind: He thought that another man fathered the child she carried. Mama was six months pregnant with my beautiful sister, Dora. Once again, my mother suffered horrible abuse because of a lie someone believed about her.

Mama would take weeks to recover. Her face swelled in misshapen lumps. Both eyes were shut in their bloody hollows, and her body was so bruised that she lay in one place for days. But we had to move. The head of the migrant camp was kind but firm. Mama wouldn't be working for a long while.

When Mama could sit up and speak, some of the ladies got together and told her about a house in Tulare. It was located on a ranch where she might work in the fields when she was well enough.

The five of us and Mama moved to the ranch and into a shed that had once housed chickens. It had a little kerosene stove, and at night I stared at stars through cracks in the tin roof, remembering Mexico. We had run full circle and met the same humiliation again. We were as poor as when we lived in the little shack in Mexico, when I trespassed the border with lunch for Fernando. In fact, we were poorer.

As soon as Mama was able, she took a job with the owner of the ranch doing domestic work. I worked picking oranges and babysat my four siblings — and then came Dora.

No Easy Road

❧ ❧ ❧

When I was 10 years old, I realized that a person who moves to America must know the workings of two currencies or live a handicapped life. One is the dollar. I learned the denominations by heart. The other medium of exchange is the English language; I applied myself to learn it in elementary school. And I worked hard to teach English to my brothers and sisters, too, so that they could survive on their own. Requiring an interpreter is like hobbling on a crutch.

In elementary school I was surprised to learn that many children in our city were worse off than me. It wasn't that they were poorer, but something had weakened them until they had no desire to compete. My family kept moving forward in the face of disaster. In our lives every spiteful word, every horrendous event strengthened our resolve to adjust, survive, learn, then excel when opportunity presented itself.

When Mama made Pedro our father, we moved to a house in the Central Valley, and I started to attend a school in an area that most people would call a ghetto. Pedro was a man that Mama respected, and he worked hard. They teamed up to move up the American ladder of success.

But in our low-rent neighborhood, stronger street kids forced me to grovel on the playground or parking lot.

"On your knees! Now pray to me, filthy Mexican!"

They invented perverse ways to instill fear in younger

children and taught us a vile hierarchy of race. Mexicans who barely spoke English were slaves — unless they joined a gang. Gang life salvaged self-respect and gave a boy or girl an identity that the ghetto stripped away.

But Mama said no.

"Gangs will destroy you in the end, Ramon. We fight a different way!"

"But I'm not weak like they think I am," I told her.

Mama looked hard into my serious brown eyes. "This will pass, Ramon. Endure, mi hijo. Endure."

It wasn't enough for me to "endure."

In elementary school, and later in middle school, I *had* to fight — in my own way. I respected my mother's wishes and never joined a gang because my brothers and sisters would have followed my example. Instead, I placed myself between those who were too weak to fight and the street bullies who hunted them. I invited street kids to vent their hatred on me in place of diminutive, pleading Thai, Black, Chicano and mixed race children. I had seen my mother endure, but in taking the pain for others, I *prevailed.*

Before I entered school in the upscale part of town, I recognized a growing intellectual power driving me to achieve. Grasping math equations and scientific theory was like baking bread. I simply followed the directions given me by my instructors.

I accompanied dozens of other underprivileged children who were bused to the school, part of a federally mandated minority quota system. The teachers and the pupils there didn't know what to make of us ghetto kids at first — and I was a real challenge. My English was terrible, but I excelled in math. Science, too, made sense to me. At first in my classes, my teachers thought I might need remedial help because of my homemade clothing and quiet, wary demeanor. But as time passed, instructors recognized my potential and placed me in advanced classes.

The reality of Disneyland, Nintendo and swimming pools shocked my poverty-inclined brain. I made friends with middle-class children, and my bus trundled through neighborhoods where every boy had his own BMX, or mountain bike. I saw no reason that I shouldn't achieve success and that my family shouldn't enjoy the riches of America, just like my new friends.

Yet, one great barrier remained that argued against my future achievements: I was a wetback. In the back of my mind, I prepared for a bus ride back to Mexico with other illegals.

By the time I was in high school, Mama had two more children, bringing my sibling count to seven, plus myself. She was often ill and looked to me to fill the role as caregiver when Pedro couldn't cope with diapers and dinners. Door-to-door religion invaded our neighborhood on a regular basis, and I brought home an enlightened worldview straight from secular textbooks. I challenged Mormons and Jehovah's Witnesses with my new doctrine of evolution. Mama didn't care who we studied religion with, as long as they taught that God "requires children to obey parents!"

A nice lady took us to a Pentecostal church down the street sometimes, and Mama stayed home with Pedro — he didn't want anything to do with any God at all. I had no understanding of who Jesus was, and I put religion on a shelf. I opened my heart to science, philosophy and mathematics.

My biggest problem during my high school years was avoiding gangs who tried to recruit me. All my friends, whom I knew in middle school and junior high, wore their gang colors proudly. On the streets, on the way home from school, I dodged their advances — I was the geeky loner, nonviolent and bookish.

But in the classroom, *I* was the predator. Among students, I could be intellectually intimidating. I spoke fluent calculus, physics, English and Spanish. Often, my teachers put me in charge of a class when they stepped out, because I was capable and conscientious.

My instructors pressed me to go to college, but my mother and stepdad needed me. I graduated from high school when I was 19 and settled into work in a migrant camp, helping Pedro, who suffered heart problems. I attended a junior college where placement counselors suggested that I pursue a short career like mechanics or landscaping — I think I fit their stereotype of a poor Mexican field hand. Chico, on the other hand, traveled the path of academics and landed a full-time teaching position by the time he was 22!

I took classes at the local college while I worked at the orchards with my stepdad. My instructor called me into his office after several months. "Ramon, have you ever considered going to the state university? You grasp the theory of mechanics, and your aptitude for math is extraordinary."

I was surprised by his assessment. I was the clumsiest mechanic in the class. Wrenches never seemed to fit my hands right.

"I'll help you any way I can to get into Fresno," he said.

I told him I appreciated his kindness, but that I couldn't see any way I could keep up my farm work and my difficult studies at Fresno State.

かかか

I shook my head when I opened my lunch pail. Two full roasted chickens crowded 10 burritos inside. I sat in a little white van that my mother had purchased for me, eating and hoping that no one parked in front of me. I had a mortal fear of backing up; I could never seem to synchronize the clutch pedal with the van's three-speed column shift lever. On the freeway, I often lurched into the median, desperately trying to locate the next higher gear, while impatient, honking commuters swerved out of my way.

And I was training to be a mechanic.

I finished up the last burrito and waddled off to class. Mama was still fully invested in my life — and she was worried.

"Ramon, you are 21 years old. You're gay! You never

go out with girls. You must be. Are you gay, mi hijo? Tell me …"

Over and over she tried to set me up with young women she knew, but my life was as crammed as my lunch box! I worked every day in the orchards or fields, helped with my brothers and sisters and then took general education classes at the local college. Couldn't Mama see that I had no room for a woman in my life?

And then there was my dream: A little boy ran into my arms, brown-skinned, with raven-black hair and laughing eyes. A voice said to me, "Ramon, this is your son."

"Mama, this dream tells me I'm not gay!"

"A dream! That's ridiculous. You can't have a *son* until you have a wife! Don't you know the way it works?"

"I know, I know. Don't worry about me." The dream reinforced what I knew about myself. I wasn't gay, no matter who thought so.

Mama saved enough money to put a down payment on a small plot of ground and an old farmhouse — the very first home she ever owned. We all moved in, and soon my brothers and sisters populated makeshift pens with a menagerie of animals. Just down the hill, within view of Mama's new home, sat the little tin-roof chicken coop we had lived in years before. It stood as a monument to our toil and tears.

The farmhouse needed repairs, and I gathered tools to replace the porch and cabinets. Neighbors and friends inspected my work, and soon I had paying projects around Tulare stacking up. Whenever I worked in the neighborhood, a little boy named Tomas pedaled up to help me, and I saw myself in his determined eyes. I welcomed his company and taught him how to handle woodworking tools. He worked long hours with me, and soon he was as indispensable as my power saw.

I also saw kindness in Tomas. He and another boy used to work for a woman with diabetes who lived on our street. They used to massage her legs and feet when they fell asleep. Kindness was a quality that I saw in my mother, too, as far back as our days in the Mexican border town. She had handed out morsels of food to the hobos who lived near the railroad tracks, though we were nearly as destitute as they.

Where did kindness come from? Or love? Were they simply neurological impulses gathered in the brain and randomly acted upon?

I had dismissed God as a crutch needed by elderly women and fearful ninos. My mind was filled with images of goo turning to invertebrates; from invertebrates to vertebrates; from vertebrates to primates; and from primates to humanity with complex emotions.

I was no longer an ignorant Mexican immigrant. At 19, I had become a citizen of the United States, thoroughly indoctrinated in secular thought taught by professors.

One day as Tomas and I nailed trim to a doorway, my little sister skipped into the house. "Ramon! I've found your wife! I found your wife, Ramon!"

"I never lost her, sis," I told her, but I *was* curious.

Later, as I ate lunch at Tomas' house with his family, I

met the potential woman of my (mother's) dreams. She was Tomas' skinny, shy sister, Carmen. With her fluffy black hair, she was not what my mind envisioned for a wife.

Oh, what a difference one year can make.

Carmen came home from visiting relatives, and she had *grown.* I was too busy to pay much more attention than staring whenever she came to see Tomas, but one day my protégé helped break the ice for me to officially court Carmen.

Tomas and I had been digging a septic tank hole, and my wiry helper accidently slammed the edge of a shovel into my head. I was out cold for a few seconds before I climbed out of the hole and stood, like a part-butchered hog, dazed and bleeding. In an emergency room at the hospital, I fell asleep because of the pain, and when I roused awake, someone held my hand. It was Carmen. She had sneaked to town to be with me, against the wishes of her strict father.

Carmen was 19 and I was 23 when we were married by her priest at their church. I bowed my head, but only out of respect for tradition. A Creator did not exist for me. And in the first year of our marriage, I would have called it mala suerte (bad luck) when a Holstein cow changed the direction of our lives.

I had been running heavy equipment at a dairy, and along the highway on a foggy night, I slammed into a dairy cow that stopped my pickup like a brick wall. My foot and shoulder sustained broken bones, and a section of my vertebrae was crushed. I lost my job, and with my wife and baby son (brown-skinned with laughing eyes), we scavenged for cardboard around town to sell to a salvage yard.

Carmen felt like we were scraping the bottom of the barrel in our first trial together, but my troubles seemed insignificant as I reflected on my past. I could do anything! I was a self-made hombre. I had no need for any higher power to help me prevail. In fact, every beating that life gave me simply made me *stronger.*

My brother Daniel worked at a local restaurant and let me in the back door to train me in kitchen work. It took a few days for the manager to notice me.

"Who in the h*** are you?" he asked, and Daniel said that I was his brother.

He looked over my work for a little while, then asked, "He getting paid, Daniel?"

"No, sir."

The manager smiled a little in my direction. "You're hired. Come to my office and get the paperwork."

In less than a year, I was managing a department of the kitchen staff. But I diligently avoided my counselor at the local college who encouraged me to apply to the state university and pursue a degree. I had a family to support, and I focused on the job at hand, to make it a success.

One day the counselor called me. "I've made an appointment for you to interview for enrollment. Remember the entrance exam you took months ago? You scored very highly! Ramon, you need to go. I'll even pay for diapers and a rental car for your transportation. Just commit to go!"

At my interview at the university, the counselor told me, "Ramon, you're going to be a teacher. And this is how you will do it …"

ॐ ॐ ॐ

How did I get here?

I had to ask myself this question sometimes as I collaborated with principals to evaluate the afterschool program for the school district. In two years, I had been promoted from inexperienced substitute teacher for special ed children to Director of the After School Program. Many of my 150 students were immigrant children, and my staff included untrained educators growing into full-fledged teachers.

No one wanted to take on the troubled, grant-starved program, so I grabbed the opportunity with both hands and made decisions guiding the whole system. It became my launching pad to a teaching career.

At every school I taught in, I found favor with principals and teachers. They studied my methods of gaining trust from my students to instruct them. Yet during my three intense years trying to achieve tenure as a schoolteacher, my home life was falling to pieces. My academic world replaced my wife and children, and Carmen slipped into a deep depression.

"I've lost you, Ramon. You've left me behind."

"Don't be crazy, Carmen. I'm working hard for all of us!" But I knew she was right. I spent less and less time with my family, and I was seduced by lofty objectives presented in academia.

"We need to go to church, Ramon. As a family. Can we?"

Carmen wasn't the only one who had been asking me to find peace in religion. My brother Chico had made a forceful decision to follow Jesus the rest of his life. I had ridiculed him over joining a club for illiterates and zealots. Then my mother made a commitment to this Jesus whom I had never respected because he let himself be killed. How could he be the God of the universe, like the Bible said?

I distanced myself more and more from my family, until Carmen decided to move away to her parents' home, taking my two precious children with her.

Only her family's deep Catholic beliefs about the unpardonable sin of divorce prevented Carmen from filing papers. After weeks of sinking into a crater of depression, Carmen called me. "Please, Ramon. Come and get us."

Before I made a decision, I visited Mama to seek her moral support.

"Ramon," she said, "go fight for your family."

On the table beside her lay an open Bible. For months she had been going to a church where Chico preached. I couldn't fathom what had come over her! My powerful mentor had thrown away her self-reliance and humbled herself before Jesus.

"Mama, she's six hours away. And I've been up for almost 24, working on school papers."

"You *go*, Ramon. I'll pray for you."

I never shirked my responsibilities, and I wasn't about to let Carmen ruin my record. I drove to her parents' home, arriving with a cracked windshield and brush imbedded in my bumper. Somewhere I had wandered off the road and didn't remember where. I crashed on a bed with my two children when I got there.

It had been a hellish few weeks for my son, Carlos, my daughter, Lori, and Carmen. They had witnessed an assault by a knife-wielding cousin. My daughter had recoiled into a shy place, completely changed from her normal buoyant self. Carmen was a worse mess than when she left, and I despised her.

I warned her not to leave, and she rejected me! Now I have to pick up the pieces — and work long hours at school, too!

Someone spoke to me: "You can rid yourself of this burden for good, if Carmen goes crazy." In a flash I pictured life without Carmen.

Then a voice said, "*Bury* her! You can destroy her. She hurt you. Look what she did to your children! It's your turn now. *She must pay for the disgrace she has brought to your family!*"

My grandmother had listened to this same voice when she beat her daughter senseless; it was the same "spirit" my stepfather, Fernando, heeded when he cut Mama with a knife …

"NO! I've always stood up for my family. I cannot bury her!"

And in the end, it was Carmen who helped me cross the border to freedom and enlightenment that saved my self-righteous soul.

ﾊｦﾊｦﾊｦ

Maybe Carmen can sing or something. Church will be good for Carlos and Lori, too.

Some people drank to deaden the pain of life. Others took drugs. I saturated myself with my teaching career to block out any angst. I was glad that Carmen discovered a crutch to help her regain her psychological balance.

I didn't mind going to the little Pentecostal church pastored by Ricardo, my brother Chico's mentor and friend. I enjoyed wrestling with the intellectual challenges that "God's word" delivered through Ricardo and Chico's preaching. At times, a peculiar light touched my presuppositions. Jesus was a historical figure, still dead to me, but I could see that his religion was helping people.

Drug addicts were testifying to losing their addictions when they gave up their lives to Jesus. Drunks walked straight and true after surrendering themselves to God. As for Carmen, she was a new creation that I could quantify, classify and analyze empirically every day. The change in her was *uncanny*.

If there was a God, these misfits really needed him.

Some were real crybabies, who prayed for minor problems in their lives. God probably appreciated that a strong person like myself associated with them.

For my family's sake, I attended services, painted walls or repaired the church van. I was making Mama proud. I was as good a Christian as any of them, and I had never even spoken to their Jesus.

Carmen had taken employment at a restaurant, and one Sunday after church she was scheduled to work an afternoon shift. When she left, Carlos and Lori read books in the living room while I headed for the kitchen to make lunch.

Before I reached the refrigerator, I slammed into a cerebral fence that stopped me cold.

An acute sense that my soul was separating from my physical body overwhelmed me. A thought reverberated in my head: *Ramon, this is your future. Your body is going to decompose. Where will your soul end up?*

Whoa. I need to know the answer to this question.

I had never opened a Bible to actually read it before, but I owned one. It lay in the trunk of my Taurus, dilapidated and worn from years of neglect. Chico had given it to me when I first started taking the family to church, three years before.

I smuggled the Bible past the kids and sat down at the kitchen table.

The first verse I read was: "If any man be in Christ he is a new creation …" and I knew that this was talking about my soul.

In my years of academic study, I had never seriously considered that my soul might live on after I died. My professors believed that God only existed in a person's mind, and at death something turned out the lights.

Suddenly I pondered over evidence that I had ignored. I developed a new thesis at the kitchen table, as I read the Bible.

At the instant I was conceived (when the male sperm met the female ovum), I had no idea my life began. I had no knowledge that my father existed. Nine months later, I was born, and my father abandoned me before I even knew him.

I grew up without a single photograph or old movie to prove my father was real — but to deny that he existed was irrational. I could not analyze it scientifically, but my father's activity (me) proved his existence.

Carmen authenticated God's influence in my family — she was fully restored from a mental collapse. People at Chico's little church had been healed from addictions, and they credited Jesus for their recovery, too.

And, unlike my absent father, God had given me a very detailed picture of himself — a historical, supernatural album lay before me on the kitchen table. The Bible's description of my soul resonated with my thesis, and I paused for a few seconds. The same voice that set me to thinking about my destiny spoke again.

I am looking for a family that will follow me.

Jesus had willingly died to pay for my past indifference and selfishness. All I had to do was follow his plan for my life. Not only was God real, but I could feel his son, Jesus, inside me!

I immediately knew that I had to teach these life-changing truths to my children. I took my old yellow Bible into the living room and opened up a discussion with my beloved class of two.

The next few days were peculiar in that I hid my new commitment to God from my wife. I didn't want her to see me teaching Carlos and Lori, because I felt humbled. After all our arguments about attending church and about Jesus, she had been right all along.

In the following weeks, after a thorough family discussion, we chose a church where we all could grow spiritually.

ॐॐॐ

I speak two languages (other than Spanish and English) to communicate the love of Jesus: I interpret Poverty so that people can understand those who live in ghettos; I translate Academia so that people can empathize with those who mistakenly believe that education is the way of discovering purpose.

Only Jesus can truly enrich the mind. Only Jesus can save the eternal soul.

For a Mexican child who crosses the border illegally, a knock on the door at home is terrifying. Every day at school might be his last activity in the Promised Land, if he is discovered.

For 13 uneasy years, I stressed over my deportation while I pursued my vision of the American dream. Now the experience energizes me to use every moment wisely as I follow Jesus Christ. I am detached from this world as only a former illegal immigrant comprehends — *my citizenship is in heaven!*

MANTLE OF LOYALTY
The Story of Jean
Written by Richard Drebert

The imposter was tall, lanky and a brunette. She could manhandle a Kenworth truck like me. Soon she would move into my house and sell crystal meth to my customers. She would tuck my babies into bed, and they would believe that her tender kisses were mine. After I was dead, she would sleep in my bed — with my husband. They had it all planned.

My husband, Frank, wasn't very subtle. I noticed right away that my driver's license was missing. He had slipped it out of my purse for her to use. And according to Frank's brother, Harry, she was spending a lot of time at the freight depot where my husband worked.

"She's the spittin' image of you, Jean. I thought it was *you* walkin' into the cold storage. But no way she's as tough as you are …"

Harry laughed at this, and he hopped back a step in mock fear. I felt like decking him, but flashed a humorless smile instead.

He was built just like Frank: broad-shouldered, naturally powerful without a single hour in the gym. Harry still savored a favorite memory of me shattering his big brother's jaw with a Mason jar.

Frank had never called me a b**** again.

And Harry had it right. No way my "replacement" was a bad a** like me. I hated to think how this woman had wrapped Frank around her little finger. Lately I noticed his sideways glances at me when he thought I wasn't looking. He seemed to loathe me.

Right after I moved in with Frank, our Ray was born, and I proved my whole family *wrong*! I cherished my baby. I had even stopped snorting crank when I was pregnant and waited months after my second child, Marie, was born before taking up the straw again.

When the kids were old enough to travel, Frank started long-haul trucking, and we hit the interstates from California to Florida, a happy couple jacked up on meth with the kids in the sleeper.

But when Marie and Ray reached school age, I put my foot down.

"I'll hold down the fort at home while you stay on the road, hon."

I became a homemaker, waking up to Sesame Street, cooking and making beds — while meth customers came and went like our house was a corner pharmacy. When Frank was home between legitimate truck runs, we smuggled eight-balls (1/8-ounce bags) of crystal meth (crank) from Sacramento. At home in Exeter, we cut (diluted) the meth with baking soda, chalk, talc … whatever powder we had, to stretch our dope and sell to clients.

We were a typical dysfunctional California family when Frank was home. We partied together, leaving the kids with my grandmother or mom, and beat on each other during our extreme meth highs or lows. When Frank rumbled out of the driveway in his Kenworth, a cloud of dread settled over me: I worried that narcotics agents were watching our house.

What if I got busted? I couldn't handle the thought of prison time, the way our meth customers described it. I snorted more and more crank to ascend higher than my paranoia, and my addiction jammed the throttle toward an inevitable break from reality.

No one believed me when I told them about Frank's plan to murder me and insert my evil twin at home. I harbored my terror alone, and I recalled the day when my paranoia shifted into high gear.

One morning I stood before a full-length mirror fingering my jutting ribcage. My dilated brown eyes rolled and darted in sunken hollows, and nervous tics amplified the desperation in my skeletal face. I couldn't feel my biceps anymore, and my thighs had atrophied, too. Who was this woman in the looking glass? Before going out, I padded my frame with several pairs of quilted shirts and pants to try and look like the Jean that Frank once loved.

"Frank, I can't do crank anymore. It's killing me. Ya know?"

"Sh**, Jean! Just eat more. Or do a line. You'll feel better."

"But, baby, I really need to quit dope. For the kids' sake. And I *can't* kick it if we deal here at home …"

"Look." Frank took my hands in his. "We gotta good

thing goin', and we need the money. And … I need my own stuff."

I lit up a few cigarettes with shaky fingers instead of eating dinner. After feeding the kids, I snorted away my fit of logic and felt invincible again. I didn't sleep that night. The next morning I drove the kids to kindergarten and forgot all about eating lunch before picking them up again.

At McDonald's I sat at a sticky plastic table watching my 4 and 5 year old play on a colorful obstacle course. I nibbled absently at their chicken nuggets. The raucous little playground looked and sounded like the interior of my brain: Creatures climbed nets and swam in a pool of dirty multi-colored balls.

Suddenly I couldn't sit anymore. I had to move and headed outside for a smoke. I watched through a window at Marie and Ray scooting down a bright-orange slide and noticed a young couple nearby "studying" me. They glanced at my kids.

Hadn't I seen them before somewhere?

Frank had hired them! They were following me. I scooped up my struggling, crying kids and loaded them into the car, leaving their shoes and my "pursuers" in a cloud of exhaust.

How did they know where I was?

Of course.

Back home in every room the house I checked lamps thoroughly for bugs. Then the telephones. I tore through the couch cushions and ripped up parts of the carpet and walls. Frank had planted eavesdropping devices *somewhere* ...

"If I turn up dead, you'll know. Frank and that woman did me in," I warned my friends.

If enough people heard about my impersonator, maybe she would fail to work her evil magic and erase me from my babies' hearts.

ॐॐॐ

Fiercely competitive at 12, I played first base and swung a bat with the power of most senior boys.

"Safe!"

My headfirst dive on home base had upended the catcher who fumbled the softball. I picked myself up off the dirt, feeling a satisfying sting from deep scrapes across my arms and belly. The softball bounced off the chain-link backstop, and the grandstand erupted in cheers.

I would add another Monarch win to my collection of medals. Mine was the deciding run in the ninth inning, and my Exeter High School teammates slapped my back red before we trotted across the diamond to shake hands with the downcast losers.

Losers. Not long ago, I felt like them. Never again ...

On the diamond, the racetrack and basketball court, a forceful self-awareness overpowered my childhood timidity. Now I challenged myself to endure the pain of sprints and pushups, to excel in any sport I chose. Coaches jockeyed for the chance to sign me up for their teams, and

I reveled in the acceptance, the attention, the sense of accomplishment.

"Great game!" I said, grinning, to our shortstop. The locker room rocked with Elton John, and I packed my sweaty blue and gold uniform in a sports bag.

Basketball season was coming up, and I had just reassured another coach that I was playing for her again this year as center. With long, sure strides I headed to a line of jocks boarding a bus that delivered us home. Away from my peculiar family, I dominated every key on the court of life. Any direction I looked, undefended goals invited me to score.

I arrived home, and the bus' double doors squeaked open. I bounded out, then stopped dead at a ramshackle gate. Filing away pleasant memories of my victory on the diamond, I crossed a threshold of smothering disorder.

We had two bedrooms to accommodate my two brothers, a sister and me. My stepdad wasn't home from work yet, but Mom was — on the couch. She nodded with half-closed eyes. It wasn't meth this time, I could tell. She seemed woozy. Must be pot.

I turned down the TV blaring about beauty cream and headed for the refrigerator. I grabbed a container of Sunny D and glanced at our grandstand of clutter: unwashed plates, dirty pots and empty boxes of macaroni and cheese, helter-skelter knives, forks, spoons. I washed the crust from a cup and poured.

Sitting at a small Formica table, I savored the sweetness in my throat, blocking out rancid kitchen odors, and pondered my life up to now. Funny. I had no memory of my kindergarten years or early grade school. It seemed that I was born a 13 year old.

My stepdad, Buck, had joined our untidy, disorganized lives when I was about 8, and I could thank him for teaching me what it meant to *endure* physical pain. His beatings had prepared me to accept burning muscles and sore joints for the sake of my sport.

Mom was better than she used to be. She wasn't as wild and crazy with men and crank as when she was younger and unattached. She lay on the couch most of the time and didn't deal drugs much anymore.

Yes, things were a little better since I was older. I seldom found maggots crawling in the sink from old garbage, because I kept ahead of the creeping filth. Of course, Buck never lifted a meaty finger. And the four of us kids — we adapted: to the neglect, to the crank our mother snorted, to Buck's boozy fits of rage.

It was just who we were at *home.*

Yet, whenever our family rented a new house in Exeter or Visalia, my gramma, like a bright, comforting star, never failed to appear. Gramma Sue always lived somewhere nearby, providing a spic-and-span haven for us kids and Mom, too. Gramma had been our guardian long before Buck staggered onto the scene.

Snuggled in blankets upon her living room floor, I watched her little TV with my brothers and sisters, feeling safe and cared for — unlike at home. Gramma said that my real dad left us when I was 5, after getting some other woman pregnant. After Dad left, Mom began partying like she had a death wish and dealt drugs to pay for her habit.

Gramma had stepped in and cared for us four kids and often for my strung-out mama, too. Even in her late 60s, as weary as she was, I knew that Gramma would never let me down. Her loyalty to me demonstrated a kindness in my life, as foreign as breakfast before school.

తతతత

I grew up a tomboy, a loner, picked on for my disheveled, unkempt appearance. At first, my backward demeanor invited sneers from peers and unwanted attention from bullies. And every thrashing I received at home from Buck, or from girls behind some school building, fueled an aggression that simmered below the surface until ignited years later in combat.

In the meantime, I grew into Jean, the athlete. She was fearless. Confident. Taking on all comers, and in junior high school, even Buck was impressed by me. My prowess on the basketball court or baseball diamond pleasured him somehow, and he came to my practices. But deep down, I harbored a fear of Mom's powerful significant other.

"You elbowed that big girl, and she was hurtin'. Got it past the referee, though!"

I was starved for acceptance and love, and Buck's warm accolades soaked into me like I was an inviting sponge. I loved that I pleased him, and I coveted the cheers of a crowd after a swish or a homerun. I built my self-worth upon what other people thought about me.

In my offseason, I roared up and down our rural streets, lined with mobile homes and weathered rentals, on a 250 Kawasaki motorcycle that Buck bought me. The boys in the neighborhood included me in their mud-ball games, and I tackled as hard and bloody as any of them. Where other girls used fashion and flirting to gain favor with boys, I became one of the guys, just as tough as they were — and if anyone doubted it, I enjoyed proving my grit.

Sometime when I was in junior high school, Mom inched close to a mental breakdown, and my cousin Vanna took her to church. Buck was his surly, beer-swilling self around home and refused to go, but Mom demanded that we kids attend a little white Pentecostal church down the street. At home she nailed up pictures of Jesus after getting "saved," and she gave up her Ouija board and quit dabbling in the occult. She started telling everyone about a life-altering, frightful demonic visitation.

"I went to church that very next Sunday, and preacher Bob called me out," my mother explained. "He said, 'Sister, the devil stood by your bed, and it is his desire to kill you …' And it was true! I knew that God would protect me if I gave my life to Jesus."

When Mom brought Gramma Sue to church, Gramma Sue went to the front and prayed for Jesus to be in her life, too. After that, Mom's TV at home rocked with Katherine Kuhlman and the PTL Club. Cousin Vanna was elated, but I hung back, leery of anything Mom was into.

But there had to be something to it — Mom had kicked her drug addiction. She quit crank and pot, cold turkey. Now she never missed church and spent a day each week vacuuming and cleaning up after Sunday church services. Sometimes I helped her, and while dusting the old wood pews in the sanctuary, I felt drawn to the altar in front of the pulpit. It was "spiritual" up front, where the pastor paced back and forth with his big black Bible balanced in his hand.

A scene in a church skit had fastened upon my soul sometime when I was little: A judge in a black robe wrested a baby from a mother's hands, and it was delivered to heaven while the mother was sentenced to hell. The alien idea about an afterlife had shaken me, and I knew that I couldn't be good enough to reach heaven without *someone's* help.

I'd seen other people kneel at the altar and pray, and I thought I would try it. I didn't really know what to say to God, so I articulated the first thoughts that came to me.

"God, I really want children. Give me a little boy someday. And, Lord, I want a little blue-eyed blond girl, too …"

It was the first time in my life that I seriously reflected upon my destiny.

And Jesus was listening.

აააა

I stood in a row of smiling girls, stoking embers of

hatred. All of us wore our blue and gold sweats and basketball shoes. The principal had handed out the last of the medals for sportsmanship, most points scored and player of the year. We were about to leave the school podium when I confronted my teammate Dixie about a mean rumor she had started — and our whispers grew louder. Suddenly my composure burst like a water balloon.

In front of the whole assembly, I flung Dixie to the floor like a ragdoll and pummeled her over and over in quick blows to the face. I straddled her, and I felt myself yanked off of her as I screamed and landed punches on whomever I could.

My whole meltdown was recorded for posterity. A picture in the Monarch yearbook later read: "Exeter High School's First Women's Wrestling Team." As for my future in athletics, the school banned me from all sports programs.

Buck stood by me at the administrator's big oak desk, looking smug.

"I'm sorry, but you have embarrassed your school, Jean," the principal said to me, ignoring Buck in his white t-shirt. "Your behavior cannot be condoned."

On the way out of his office, my emotions unwound like a mashed softball, innards lolling out. Buck opened the car door for me, and I crawled in, dejected, suspended from school for weeks.

"I'm proud of you, girl. You stood up for yourself. The h*** with the d*** school."

I stared at Buck's tanned grinning face, confused. It seemed that any door for scholarships or friendships had slammed in my face. As for the rage inside me, I felt it rise into my chest and fill my head.

Buck was right! The h*** with them. The h*** with the whole stinking world.

We moved to Visalia from Exeter, and despite her religious experience, Mom descended into a deep depression. I felt whipped and angry, but I had one consolation: My new school was chockfull of angry kids from dysfunctional families, just like me. They were the smokers who congregated just outside the school grounds, planning parties.

The school jocks wouldn't talk to me, and their contempt opened up a vista of friendships with other misfits. The smokers welcomed me into their club of misery. If anyone disrespected me, I beat him or her down, and my fights elevated me to the status of celebrity. In junior high, I experienced sex for the first time, and I basked in a counterfeit approval that fed my young heart.

My reputation as a bad a** grew larger than life when I cruised the boulevards with several guys, picking out targets.

"How 'bout him, Jean?"

"H***, yeah! Let me out." I tossed my bottle of Southern Comfort on the seat and threw open the car door before the ride stopped. I softened up my quarry with a few urban insults, then pounded the muscular youth to the ground before he knew what hit him. Buck had often surprised me with a fist in the face, when I least expected it. My victim lay dead still before I dismounted his chest. We sped away, laughing, and I upended my whiskey bottle.

"Find someone else!"

Rock n' roll blasted out our open windows as I hunted.

My school wasn't pleased about my grades or my notoriety. I fought in math class. Someone picked a fight during drama class, and I finished him off. No one wanted me around, for fear that I might explode.

Sometimes I walked to my gramma's house for lunch, and she always had the door locked tight, even though she knew I was coming. Mom had often locked a door if she was snorting or bagging up dope. What was Gramma doing?

Her eyes were bloodshot and red when she opened the door, and it startled me seeing her in obvious pain. "Gramma! What's wrong? What is it?"

She always smiled away my questions and sat me down for a sandwich and soup. "Nothing. Everything's going to be okay, Jean. I love you, sweetheart."

Buck moved in and out of Mom's life, and together they concluded that my real father had earned a dose of my rebellion. I was, after all, *his* kid. So, Decatur, Illinois, became my new stomping grounds for a few months — until I beat up my half-sister.

My father had seemed genuinely pleased when his tall, dark-haired, athletic daughter invaded his life. I felt truly wanted for a short time. But his wife, Minerva, wasn't happy. She was raising four children before I dropped into her lap, and I was a high-maintenance adolescent.

I kept my anger bottled up pretty well at the beginning of my stay, but my half-sister, Cindy, was about my age and jealous.

I was just as jealous, and when I stretched out a blouse that I borrowed, she gave me a verbal tongue-lashing. I turned it into a physical confrontation, and my older half-brother had to hold me back from beating her to a pulp.

Minerva was screaming, "Stop! Jean! No more. You hear?"

Cindy sniffled on the couch, milking her mother's sympathy, and I screamed back, "Minerva, you stay out of my face, or you'll get it next!"

Dad came home and huddled with Minerva in the bedroom. He was boiling mad, and I hoped he wouldn't unleash his 6-foot-4, 280 pounds on me. It wouldn't be pretty …

I listened at the door. Minerva's shrill voice rose, and her nails scratched the chalkboard of my heart: "Jean's gotta go, Ted. I can't deal with her. She's going to hurt somebody."

Dad's silence spoke loud and clear. I figured that he didn't want me, either. A sense of abandonment stuck in my throat, and I packed my suitcase. I wouldn't stay where I wasn't wanted. I demanded a ride to the airport.

At the terminal, Dad nearly crushed me in his bear hug. He grabbed my shoulders and said, "Jean, why are you leaving?"

I couldn't help brushing stinging tears away as I told him what I overheard.

"You don't want me, Dad …"

My father's eyes swelled red, too, and man-sized tears drizzled down his cheeks. It reassured me, knowing that he was torn to pieces, too.

But reality sets its jaws like a pit bull: Dad had screwed up his life 15 years before when he abandoned his family for another woman. He was paying the price — and so would I.

Back in Visalia, I settled in at home, and sometimes Buck put himself in charge of a case of beer and us kids, while Mom was away. I was banned from leaving the house at night, and every evening I closed myself into my bedroom, cranking up the music — then climbed out the window to find a party.

Buck hated to be made the fool. When he discovered that I snuck out, he planted himself by my bedroom window with a six-pack; sure enough, after a few hours, I popped my head inside. I stopped, wide-eyed, waiting for the next shoe to drop, but he just smiled.

"Jean, Jean … just use the front door."

Relieved, I trotted to the porch thinking up excuses. After all, Buck *wasn't* my real father. What right did he have to …

Our front door stood wide open, and I walked through, into a rock-hard fist that knocked me stone cold. Seconds later, I stirred, half in and half out of the doorway. I curled into a ball to protect my soft parts from Buck's steel-toed boots. Buck had been drinking and fuming nearly all night, *waiting*.

The cops came, and I ended up in the hospital. Buck got a warning. The police officers said that I deserved what I got. Who knows what my stepdad told them. I was too dazed to report anything more than groans. It was the last time Buck beat me. But other men in my life would take up where he left off, feeling as justified for their violence as he.

❧❧❧

Mom found plenty of customers for her new marijuana distribution business — in the red-light district of Los Angeles. Her self-imposed isolation from kind, loving people at church, her mental breakdown and her reclaimed addiction had shipwrecked her fledgling faith in God. My mother fell back into a familiar cesspool — while catching hold of her teenage children's hands, one by one, pulling them under with her.

When I couldn't find a dope supplier, Mama spotted me a few joints to get me through the days. She understood my need better than anyone. I despised my last year of high school and quit two semesters before graduating, but I had a good reason: I fell in love.

I met a man eight years my senior while partying, and I moved into his apartment. And he loved me, too — for almost a year. Where Mom enabled me to find comfort in drugs, Charley got me hooked on the competitive thrill of snorting more and more crank to keep up with him. He had me beat by a mile at first. But no one ever bested Jean for long. Before he dumped me, I could stay high longer than him.

My grandmother had let Charley and me stay with her for a time, after we got evicted for trashing his apartment, as druggies will. When Charley left me, I felt devastated and abandoned again. He was my first love, and I would have been a loyal wife, had we ever married. Gramma Sue had the same luck with men; Mom, too. Now the curse of loving the wrong man stalked me.

Months later, partying with my new lover, Frank, seemed too good to be true. Frank was a man with a chest that a woman could lean into and feel safe. He was a construction man, with hazel eyes, olive skin and dark hair with highlights from summer rays. He was well-heeled, and I respected his natural power and presence. And when I threw my weight around, testing his strength, I knew he wasn't a man to be trifled with. Other men knew it, too.

Perfect.

I was 18 and Frank was 26 when I settled into his life, like a new piece of quality furniture. I had met Frank one time, years before, when I raced up and down the street on my Kawasaki — he liked what he saw then, too. I thought I knew how to party, but Frank was *crazy.* I couldn't keep up with him, even at Charley's pace. Frank circulated in a network of meth, LSD, mushroom and crank addicts *and* suppliers.

His big connection, Caesar, lived in Sacramento, and

Frank schooled me in how to bring product home, cut it, bag it and keep his growing string of clients happy.

I was 20 when I got pregnant — and the prayer I prayed for a son at the little white church held me in custody the whole time I carried my baby. My conscience felt the touch of God, and I knew that he was answering my most intimate prayer. Still, I ran full tilt at life, tapering off the drugs and booze only until my baby was born.

With the birth of my son, an unfolding panorama of my child's future caught my attention for the first time. Fourteen months after Ray was born, my blue-eyed, blond-haired daughter, Marie, shook up my world again. Her beautiful Nordic features arrested me. The first prayer for a son might be a coincidence. But how could I explain away a blue-eyed blond girl from two dark-haired parents? God had answered my prayers *twice.* Neither of my children were planned or even wanted by Frank, but sometimes, when he wasn't high, I believe he discerned the same panorama of responsibility that I felt.

After our truckin' days ended, my drug use had skyrocketed, and paranoia bonded with malnutrition. Delusions stalked every waking moment, and often Gramma Sue babysat Ray and Marie while I snorted again and again to regain control of my life. Suicidal thoughts raked my emotions whenever I allowed myself to come down from my highs.

"Come on, Jean. Caesar called and is saving a few eight-balls for us. It'll be good to get you out of the house."

Frank opened the front door, and I walked through,

like a zombie. Two other meth heads piled into the back of our Caddy for our road trip, and I took the front seat with Frank. It was a long drive, and the thought occurred to me that Frank might have plans for my murder somewhere between Visalia and Sacramento.

It might be better for Ray and Marie if I was dead ...

No one wanted me anymore. I was a shell, with no power to change who I was. My life *should* end. I glanced at the speedometer, and Frank was driving like he did his truck: pedal to the metal. He careened onto the Sacramento exit and hit the straightaway at 85 miles per hour.

Truckin' on so many interstates, I had seen my share of deer shredded by cars and trucks. I pictured myself bouncing, unconscious on the pavement, ground up by vehicles, multiple times ...

So easy. And it would all be over.

I reached for the door handle and squeezed ...

At that instant, I felt gentle fingers touch every corrupted nerve in my body, a sensation more profound than any earthly rush. I knew immediately that it was Jesus, because of the shout in my mind. A surge of authority, love and consuming empathy paralyzed my will to die.

I'll help you. I am right here. Just stop using drugs.

I started weeping convulsively, like a child being comforted after her first bike wreck. Frank never asked what was wrong. He just slowed down a little, unsure of what was going on. I felt the hand of the young woman in the backseat on my shoulder, but couldn't answer when she asked why I was crying.

I think Frank and our two passengers were glad to get to Caesar's house so they could snort away *my* angst. My bawling really brought everyone down for the last few miles. We spent the night at Caesar's and hauled our dope to Exeter the next day.

A dream my first night back home helped me interpret exactly where I was in life: I stood in a deep mud hole, buried up to my neck. I could see Frank and all my drug friends around me, staring, but not moving an inch to pull me out. Suddenly Frank walked over to me, looked down and hopped over my head, laughing at me. I tried to move my limbs, but the miry clay held me paralyzed in place.

I could see and hear everything going on around me, but I was *trapped.*

All I could move were my eyes, and a sudden movement above my head drew my attention. An arm descended to the mud hole, reached into the mire and grasped me, gently lifting me from the pit. God's hand carefully cleaned me off, and then he nudged me in a direction.

The same voice I heard in the car said, "It's your grandmother's prayers that kept you, Jean."

Now I knew exactly why Gramma's eyes always looked so swollen and red when she came to the door. She was praying for Jesus to save her bad a** little granddaughter.

๑๑๑

I can only imagine what Pastor Donna thought when she met me for the first time. Cousin Vanna hauled me — boney and emotionally drained — to a little Pentecostal church called the Gospel Lighthouse Training Center and introduced me. The two women hugged me and led me in a weepy prayer that changed me forever. I unconditionally offered my skin-over-bones body, my paranoid mind and starving spirit to Jesus.

While the kids bunked at Gramma's house, Vanna let me stay with her for a few days. Every whiff of drug addiction vanished, and my appetite returned. My paranoia left me completely after a week of praying and reading the Bible. I still looked like an emaciated wreck, but inside me the maggots weren't crawling in and out of garbage anymore. God had cleaned me and taken up residence in my soul.

I stopped dealing drugs with Frank, and he wasn't happy. I freaked him out — this new woman he lived with read her Bible while he snorted crank. When Frank partied with lowlifes, I attended meetings at the Gospel Lighthouse with my kids and Vanna. Former addicts who knew me couldn't believe I had been freed from the mud hole they left me in.

And I was hungry! For all my favorite foods and for the Bible. Jesus spoke to my heart every time I read it. One verse in particular encouraged me. It was Psalm 40:2-3: "He lifted me out of the slimy pit, out of the mud and mire; he set my feet on a rock and gave me a firm place to stand. He put a new song in my mouth, a hymn of praise to our God. Many will see and fear the LORD and put their trust in him."

As for my anger issues, I learned that God powered the truck, but I had the responsibility to steer it. Frank tried to pick fights by pushing all the old buttons, but I didn't respond to his digs. I marveled that I was able to control my temper for the first time in years.

Then I went too far …

"Frank, I don't think it's right that we live together without being married. Can we make it legal?"

"H***, Jean. I don't wanna get *married*! I like things the way they are."

I prayed about my situation, and I couldn't ignore the fact that we were living without any vows before God. One morning I drove Frank to a convenience store for some smokes, and while he stood at the counter, I drove off with him staring after me.

The kids and I packed a few things and moved out to a relative's home. Ray, Marie and I prayed each morning and night that he would come home to us.

"Jesus, we want to be a family. Lord, change his mind about marriage."

Through seven years of my self-destructive behavior, Frank stuck with me — an enabler for my addiction, but also a father to my children. I felt that God wanted me to follow through with my commitment to Frank.

Meanwhile, Frank partied like an animal set free from his cage — for a while. Then, according to mutual friends, he settled into a funk. For seven months he resisted God's leading to come home to us and make things right. In that time, Jesus spoon-fed me his wisdom as I prayed and studied the Bible for hours at a time.

It would have been easy to move on with my life. But one night a dream about Frank convinced me I was on the right track. I saw Frank knocking on our front door. I opened it, and he said, "Jean, let's get married."

The next morning, as I wondered if God had given me this dream or if I had just eaten too much pizza, I heard a knock …

There Frank stood, a little sheepish. "Okay. C'mon. Let's get married, Jean."

We loaded up the kids and headed for Las Vegas, then to Disneyland for our honeymoon.

As soon as we left Fantasyland, Frank and I tangled in a life-and-death struggle of wills. Every time Frank picked up a straw for crank or got high on LSD, I experienced his anguish. I understood the pain of his addiction, and he grew to envy my God-given peace. My compassion toward him infuriated him, and I passively endured his abuse whenever our lifestyles collided.

Sometimes I prayed, "Oh, Jesus, release me from my vow to this man. Please!" But I couldn't leave Frank, because I knew my purpose in life was entwined with his. It took 11 years for God to show me the reason for my "crazy" resolve.

இஇஇ

"Get those guys out of here."

"Now, Gramma, there's no one here but us …"

"Tell those guys to leave …"

I stood with my mom in Gramma's hospital room, teary-eyed. Gramma was 72 and a diabetic. She had been on the road to recovery when she saw the angelic men in her room. In a short time, she was taken to heaven. It was her time to go.

Pastor Grimley contacted me afterward.

"I had a dream, Jean — about you. I saw your Gramma Sue handing a special garment to you before she went to be with Jesus. It was her prayer mantle (cloak), and it belongs to you now."

I knew how potent Gramma's prayers were — I was living proof. Frank was at the top of my list of prayer requests, and I made it clear to God that I expected this man to be in heaven with his children. I believed it with all of my heart, even without seeing a single positive change in Frank.

My husband had always been a gear head, rebuilding and souping up engines to run faster and better. I loved bored-out cylinders and pistons, too (I was 17 when I rebuilt my first motor). Frank began losing the natural strength that had characterized his life, and in a short time, he could barely grip a wrench. In 1998, my husband was diagnosed with cancer. After his treatments, it seemed that he would survive, but even after an organ transplant, his kidneys functioned at about 15 percent of cleansing capacity.

Suddenly, faced with his mortality, Frank searched his soul and discovered *me*. After all our struggles, I was still with him. My loyalty showed him what Jesus looked like: forgiving and willing to sacrifice for him.

Then God answered my passionate, heartfelt prayer. He sent a man into Frank's life who spoke his language.

Seth was a friend of mine who had been paroled from prison after serving a sentence for murder. The upper half of Seth's torso read like a collage of demons, women and barbed wire.

His tats told of the violent life he had lived before surrendering to God; now he was a wild, uninhibited street evangelist. While Frank read and listened to Seth's story, Jesus touched his heart. The two men became friends, and Frank offered his heart and soul to Jesus. My husband kicked his addictions and became the dad to my kids that he was destined to be.

I had my precious man of God for five years before he died in my arms at home.

After Frank's death, an old sense of abandonment crept into my soul. I downshifted to weather a bumpy road ahead: My beloved children were college age and had moved out of the house. My mother had started attending church again but still struggled with her addictions, and my brother had suddenly died of cancer at 39.

Somehow I felt disconnected from my Christian friends; I wandered into a mega-church in Visalia where no one knew me.

I settled into a job as an industrial maintenance

technician at a manufacturing plant, working swing shift (no more Sunday church), and I made new friends.

"Hey, Jean! Come with us. We're having a few drinks after work ..."

I unlocked a door that led to heartache, but I was *lonely*. I read my Bible every other day, then once a week, then not at all.

I chose parties with self-absorbed friends over fellowship with Jesus and his people. And finally, I stumbled headlong into a relationship with Carey, a man I met while on a night out with some girlfriends. He seemed to fill a jagged hole in my heart left by Frank's death and my acute *sense of failure in serving God.*

Old voices from my past roared in my ears: "You aren't worth sh**. Why not find happiness in someone you can touch?"

I tuned out the voice of God: "Jean. Never commit your heart to this man. You've been through hell already! Why would you think about marrying someone who's not sold out to Jesus?"

But I was 40 years old now, and I had my future to consider. Carey was near his retirement and had a good pension coming. We discussed keeping a nice home and plans to travel. My nightmare began soon after I said, "I do."

We discovered very few common interests — especially regarding religion. Carey couldn't stomach the little Pentecostal church that I loved, and for me, his Lutheran denomination seemed to be on spiritual life support. We compromised by attending Bethel Family Worship Center in Tulare.

Within a few months of our vows, I unexpectedly injured my lower back on the job. After a diagnosis from a specialist, he prepped me for a series of back surgeries. Sadly, the prognosis for my marriage appeared as bleak as my hope of living a pain-free life. My husband concluded that I would be an invalid as long as I lived.

Carey unemotionally analyzed the sacrifices he would need to make and came to a "reasonable" decision.

"Look, Jean. I'll be retiring soon, and I can't be saddled with someone who might end up being confined to a wheelchair. You understand ..."

I choked back tears as I remembered changing soiled bedding for my dying husband — for *years*! I had married a man who was dumping me for a healthier model.

I reined in my old rage and said, "Carey, if you think I'm going to be some invalid because the doctors say so, then you really don't know me. And remember this: If you were ever diagnosed with cancer, I'd have wiped your a** till the day you died."

Carey divorced me, anyway.

Abandoned again, I *ran* into the arms of Jesus as fast as I could limp.

One night Vanna took me to a special church service in Porterville. The speaker pointed me out in the crowd and said, "God told me to tell you that in the Bible, Jeremiah 29:11, reads, 'For I know the plans I have for you,' declares the Lord, 'plans to prosper you and not to harm you, plans to give you hope and a future.'" What encouraging words at a time I needed them most!

I began to notice these words often. I even won a bracelet with the verse on it at a drawing at a Christian concert! It became a constant reminder that God had better things in store for me.

❧❧❧

The following year, I focused all my effort upon learning what God expected me to do with the rest of my life. I had little knowledge of what church life was all about. It seemed that God kept the shepherds (pastors and teachers) and sheep (common folk, like me) in separate pens. My mind was saturated with self-doubt, and I had no idea that God could use me to be his hands for healing wounded souls.

With thorough teaching from the Bible at Bethel, clouds of mistrust and uncertainty cleared away, revealing Jesus. By absorbing the full truth in scripture over the months, God was preparing me for a major shift in my destiny.

I had always been attracted to rough-cut men, full of themselves and strutting with bravado. But after about a year of attending Bethel, my heart grew tender toward a church maintenance technician named Leo.

I told God, "Lord, you must be crazy! Take this man out of my mind. No way is this guy for me."

Leo was on staff — he was one of the shepherds. He

understood the Bible and taught it. I was learning, but took every Bible promise at blatant face value, believing like a child and blasting hell open with my prayers.

Leo and I had a foyer relationship, greeting each other politely on the way somewhere, but every time I saw the man, it seemed that God nudged me in his direction.

"Stop looking on the outward appearance, Jean. I'm seeing the man's heart — and it's a kind and generous one …"

God wouldn't give me any rest about it, so I decided to act. I asked Leo, pointblank, for a date. He said no.

I spent the next week in the dumps for humiliating myself.

I decided to ignore him at church (without much success) and implored God to take the silly attraction out of my heart. One day during worship service on a Sunday morning, I laid it on the line.

"Lord, if Leo doesn't come over and talk to me *today*, I'm moving on with my life. I'm closing the book on this one-sided 'crush' forever."

The service ended, and I put figurative blinders on as I strode resolutely out the door toward the parking lot. I believed I had simply misread God's leading …

"Jean! Wait!" Leo came trotting after me. "I can't explain it, but I couldn't let you leave without talking to you …"

I enjoyed telling Leo exactly *why* he felt so panicked. God certainly has his own peculiar ways of bringing two unsettled Jesus-loving people together.

No Easy Road

❧❧❧

In view of eternity, my wonderful marriage to Leo is only a drop in the bucket of time. Our four precious years so far are strands of an unbreakable braid of mercy in my life. God's love for me has been relentless. Unceasing.

I feel that God has catapulted me into unexplored territory. Now I head up the inner healing ministry at Bethel Family Worship Center, and I'm active in the drama team as well — even after five back surgeries.

I am on call 24/7 for Jesus and spend much of my time as a telephone minister, contacting people that God brings to mind. Sometimes these dear souls are a little surprised that Jesus is listening in. I don't wait to put them on a prayer chain — I bring their problems to Jesus on the spot. And our church celebrates the miracles:

"Jean, I'm in San Francisco with my niece. She had her baby …" I could tell that Darla fought back tears. I had spoken with her the day before, and she had asked for prayer for her pregnant niece, Cynthia. Overnight the situation had grown serious. Medics had flown the mother to an emergency medical center in the Bay Area.

"The baby was … dead, Jean. The doctors had to revive him. Now the baby's head is swelling." She paused to gain a little control. "It's the size of a football."

I was already praying silently before Darla asked, "Can you please pray for him?"

"Of course I will. Could I speak with Cynthia?"

Darla handed the phone to the weary little mother —
and I began praying with her and for her.

"Lord Jesus, Cynthia thinks that the reason her son is
ill is because you're mad at her. She thinks you are going
to kill her baby …"

I felt a deep anger at Satan, the enemy of Cynthia's
soul. I had been on the receiving end of the devil's
deceptions, too.

I gentled down my emotions to talk to the frightened
girl. "Honey, this is a lie from the devil. God isn't
punishing you. He is your Father. Jesus wants you to give
your heart to him. He loves you …"

Cynthia surrendered her life to Jesus right there.

The three of us asked God for the child's life, and an
image raced across my mind; I saw Jesus handing the baby
to Cynthia, *healed*.

"Now, declare and decree before God that your baby
will live and not die."

I felt an overwhelming peace in my soul, and I knew
the young mother felt it, too. "I know you've never sensed
the presence of God before, Cynthia, but *this* is what he
feels like. He wants you to know he's with you."

We hung up our phones, and I sat quietly alone,
feeling a deep empathy for the girl.

Ten minutes later, Darla called again.

"I just wanted you to know that the baby's head is …
normal, Jean! He's scheduled for an MRI next — the
doctors think he has brain damage due to the several
minutes he was dead. Please PRAY!"

We did, and by God's mercy, the MRI scan showed the tissue in the baby's brain to be completely healthy.

Two weeks later, before the congregation at Bethel Family Worship Center, Cynthia held her baby boy, with Darla and me standing by her side. We told her story about the healing power of God. Three women had simply believed what Jesus said in the Bible. God healed the child and saved his mother.

And I believe that Gramma is very pleased.

THE ROAD TO HEALING
The Story of Scott
Written by Karen Koczwara

Cancer.

The word hurtled toward me like a bullet and then lodged itself somewhere between my throat and my gut. Had I heard the doctor right?

Tumor. Treatment. Chemotherapy. Specialist. Tests. Urgent. I was half listening, my head spinning as I reeled in shock. I'd thought we were here for a few routine tests. How could this be happening?

Cancer. The word hit me again, this time a straight punch in the face. Other people got cancer. People on TV, people in books, people on billboards. Not people like me.

As the doctor droned on, only one thought raced through my mind: *Am I going to die?*

❧❧❧

I was born in Spokane, Washington, in 1951, the youngest of four children.

My father drove a laundry truck for a living, while my mother worked at various department stores to bring in extra income. We were a step above poor, included among the many hardworking families who stretched every last dollar to put a hot meal on the table and pay the bills. My father often came home exhausted and angry, weary after a long day of driving from shop to shop to collect dirty rags.

"Who made this d*** mess?" he hollered as he slammed the front door. He kicked off his work boots and threw them down the hallway, then sank onto the sofa to take a deep breath.

I tiptoed out of the room, not wanting to upset my father. As much as I loved him, he was known for his short temper, and often when we worked together in the garage, my smallest mistakes seemed to prompt his reprimands. I knew my father put in long hours at work to provide for our family of six, so I did my best to stay out of his hair as much as possible.

My mother worked most afternoons; when I got home from school, my brothers and sister would greet me at the door. "Mom's at work again, but she wants us to come down to the store for a milkshake," they told me.

A big smile would creep to my face. I loved visiting my mother at the department store, sitting on the high stool and slurping a thick shake from a plastic straw. But I liked it better when she was at home, baking her famous cherry pies or whipping up a batch of delicious potato salad for the Fourth of July picnic. Though she often complained about her health, my mother was the strongest, hardest-working woman I knew.

In the fall of 1968, I started my junior year of high school. My father announced he was taking a job in nearby Clarkston and moved our whole family. The timing was less than ideal for a boy my age, but I threw myself into sports and signed up for football, wrestling and baseball. I was just settling into life in our new home when we learned some devastating news: My mother had liver cancer.

"We'll take this one day at a time, and we'll beat this," my mother assured us, trying to stay brave.

But inside, I didn't feel very brave. I couldn't bear the thought of losing my mother. That fall, we moved back to Spokane, and I returned to my old high school. It was too late to sign up for sports, and I had little energy to invest in my old friends. Instead, I watched as the cancer ravaged my mother's body, transforming her from a vivacious woman to a frail, helpless being.

I tried to hide my pain, but my friends noticed the change in my demeanor.

"Man, you're not the same Scott," my old buddy told me. "What happened to the fun athletic guy we all used to know?"

I didn't feel like talking about the bitterness that overwhelmed me, the fear that seized me as I lay in bed every night, wondering if my mother was going to die.

In November that year, my mother lost her battle to cancer and passed away. It was Thanksgiving time, a season representing love, laughter, family and gratitude. Yet, I didn't feel like I had much to be thankful for anymore.

I grew withdrawn and depressed as I watched my father grieve his beloved wife and my siblings try to cope. Over the years, my mother had taken us to church on the holidays, and I'd always enjoyed the stories of Jesus from the Bible. The Sunday school teacher had shared about the baby born in a manger, the one who was God's son. I'd often thought about him as I got older and wondered if this Jesus really cared about a kid like me. I wanted to believe, but if God really cared for people as much as my Sunday school teacher said, then why had he taken my beloved mother from me?

In January 1970, my father moved us back to Clarkston again. It was the middle of my senior year, and the idea of starting over for the third time was exhausting. I intended to keep to myself, but I couldn't help notice a pretty brunette named Karen at school. We struck up a conversation one day, and within no time, we began dating. Karen was fun, interesting and sweet, and I wondered if she might be the girl I'd end up marrying someday.

That fall, my father struck up a new romance of his own and got remarried. It was difficult to see him with another woman after losing my mother.

But even more devastating was the fact that my new stepmother resented me from the start. With my siblings now grown and out of the house, I was left alone as a target for her anger.

"I don't want any of your d*** friends over here, you got it?" she snarled at me one day when I got home. "Your father didn't even tell me he had a kid still at home when we got married, and I didn't sign up for this gig. So you just keep out of my hair, you hear?"

I stormed out of the room, slamming my bedroom door behind me. I could hardly wait to move out on my own so I could get away from this woman.

My stepmother's vicious behavior continued, until one day I could not take it anymore. "You're way out of line!" I screamed at her.

"Then you're out of here," she yelled back. "Go pack your things and leave the house! You're a grown kid now!"

I waited for my father to back me up, but his eyes were vacant and unresponsive. I stomped out of the room and called my girlfriend on the phone. "I need a place to stay," I told her desperately.

"I'll see if my folks will let you stay here for a while," she said.

Karen's parents agreed to let me live with them; I was grateful for their support. Her father became like a father to me, helping me secure a job at the local pulp and paper mill. I stayed there until the following summer, when I began classes at Washington State University and moved into the dorms. I wanted to get my life back on track and be successful, but things only took a turn for the worse.

"Dude, you gonna come smoke with us tonight?" one of my buddies asked, pulling a bag of weed out of his pocket. "Got enough to go around."

I'd never smoked weed before, but I figured a little couldn't hurt. It was the 70s after all, and pot was as commonplace as long hair and bell bottoms. But the booze and the pot soon escalated to other drugs, and partying took priority over studying.

The next summer, I moved out of the dorms and into an apartment near campus, which my roommates and I decorated with black lights and wall-to-wall mattresses. At night, we lay in the dark and passed around the joint until our eyelids drooped and we fell asleep. By the end of the school year, my grade point average plummeted.

"We're going to have to ask you to leave," the admissions counselor told me with a frown. "I'm sorry, but your grades are unacceptable for our standards."

I was disappointed in myself, but I focused instead on my relationship with Karen. We married that August, and I attended a different college near our home. Though I loved life as a newlywed, my mother's death haunted me day and night. Depression sank in, and my self-esteem hit a new low. I tried visiting a psychologist, but the dark cloud still hovered over me wherever I went. *What's wrong with me?* I asked myself repeatedly. *Why can't I snap out of this funk? I have a beautiful wife and a decent life. I should be happier.*

I began comparing myself with others around me. It seemed everyone I knew, including my siblings, was more successful, better looking and more financially stable. Their homes were nicer, their cars were newer, they were more well-liked.

I tried to take control of my own life, working out at the gym for hours until my muscles rippled when I looked in the mirror. In the morning, I changed my clothes four or five times before heading out the door. I constantly worried what others thought of me and convinced myself I was not good enough. The anxiety weighed heavily on me, but I could not shake it off.

In August 1973, I returned to Washington State University, and Karen and I moved into an apartment for married students. I chose a Communication Disorder major and worked hard to get better grades. But when I wasn't studying, I partied with Karen and my friends, drinking myself into a stupor on the weekends and smoking weed again.

"Dude, there's the department lush," my friend teased when I showed up for class after a long weekend of partying.

I laughed. "Yeah, guess that's me," I replied, sinking into my seat.

Toward the end of my schooling, I signed up to work in a clinic with children and adults of all ages. I knew I couldn't be a good example with the amount of partying I did, so I cut out the weed but kept drinking on the weekends. *At least it's a start,* I told myself. *Besides, it's not like I'm an alcoholic or anything. Everyone around here parties.*

I earned my degree and started a graduate program for Speech and Language Pathology in August 1975. In July 1977, I learned of a job opening in Visalia, California.

"What do you think?" I asked Karen. "I hear it's pretty nice down there."

"We should check it out," she agreed.

Karen and I moved to Visalia that summer, and I started my first job as a speech and language pathologist.

That December, Karen gave birth to a beautiful little boy. We were both thrilled to be parents, and I thought perhaps my life was finally complete. I had a great job, a loving wife and now a child of my own. We loved our new town, and I'd finally traded in my hard-partying ways for life as an adult. I put my struggles out of my mind and focused on being the best father, husband and worker I could.

In December 1980, Karen gave birth again, this time to a little girl. We were elated to have one of each. But shortly after she was born, I learned some devastating news: Karen had been having an affair with our neighbor.

"How could you do something like that?" I cried, baffled and hurt.

"It just … happened," she confessed sadly, hanging her head. "I'm really and truly sorry. He was just lonely because he just got divorced, and … I dunno … I started spending time with him. I'm really sorry, Scott."

I didn't know what to think or do. I loved Karen and couldn't believe she'd betrayed me and our family. "Maybe it would be better if we separated for a bit, until we can sort this all out," I said with a resigned sigh. "I need to just clear my head."

Karen and I separated with the intention to repair our marriage. I continued to attend the Catholic church, which Karen had introduced me to when we first met. Most Sundays, I left just as emotionally dry as when I walked through the doors. I often thought of the Sunday school I'd attended as a child and the Jesus I'd learned about. My teacher made him sound so wonderful, like someone who could be your best friend. Did that Jesus really exist, or was God just some far-off figure in the sky we recited verses about each week?

One day, my next-door neighbor came over and asked me if I'd like to go to church with him.

"It's a nondenominational church," he explained. "Everyone is welcome, and I think you'll really like it."

What do I have to lose? I figured. My relationship with my wife was on the brink of crumbling, despite her constant plea for forgiveness. I didn't know how to sort things out on my own anymore. I needed help.

In April 1982, the church sponsored an outreach event where a popular Christian pastor spoke. He spoke tenderly about a God who loved us so much. He said that God sent his son, Jesus, to take the punishment for my wrongdoings so that I wouldn't have to. He said I could have a meaningful relationship with God by believing in what Jesus did for me and asking God to forgive me. Then I could begin a new journey with God. The world would disappoint me over and over, he added, but Jesus would never let me down if I would only have faith in him.

As the music played softly in the background, I sat frozen in my seat, letting his words sink in. I wanted to know this God the pastor talked about. All the rituals I'd performed for years in the Catholic church never showed me how to connect with God. Suddenly, it all made perfect sense. Jesus was the only way to know God.

When the pastor asked if anyone would like to begin a

relationship with Jesus by inviting him into his or her life, I came forward and did just that. My feet felt light and my heart surged with happiness as I returned to my seat. I was on my way to becoming a new man!

I began attending my neighbor's church, and for the first time in my life, I experienced God in a new and wonderful way. Karen and I reunited, but the affair still hung between us like an invisible dark cloud. The church asked me to lead a Bible study in my house, and I agreed. Each week, 20 people gathered in our living room to study the Bible.

"Thank you all for coming," I told them as we prayed together. "I am really excited about the things God is going to show us."

I loved studying the Bible and learning more about God with my new friends, and from the outside, I looked like a happy, respectable man. But inside, something still gnawed at me. Even though I knew God had forgiven me for the wrong I'd done, I couldn't quite forgive my wife for the affair. The betrayal haunted me, reminding me of my mother's death. I wanted to believe people would not let me down, that *God* would not let me down, but could I fully give up my heart in exchange for true peace?

In 1988, our church announced they were doing a mission trip to China and the Philippines. Those going would help smuggle Bibles into places where people were not allowed to talk about God or hold public church services. I prayed and decided to join the team. I felt it would be an experience of a lifetime, a way for me to stretch my faith in God and also a chance to sort out my marriage troubles. I grew excited as the date of the trip neared.

Twenty of us flew out of San Francisco, landed in Hong Kong and prepared to board a flight to Beijing. My heart raced as we entered the airport terminal; our suitcases were full of Bibles. If a security attendant stopped us, they could easily discover our smuggled goods. "Please, God," I prayed. "Let us make it through so we can bring these Bibles to those who need to know you in this country."

"Your bag is too heavy. I need you to open it," an attendant announced to a group of people in front of us.

My heart thumped louder as the attendant dug through their bags.

Miraculously, when we stepped up in line, they did not question us at all. We breathed a sigh of relief and kept walking through.

"Thank you, God," I whispered under my breath as we headed to Beijing.

We watched God provide again and again throughout the rest of the trip, from finances to circumstances. As I praised God for taking such good care of us, I wondered if he could perform the same miracles in my marriage. Things had gone from bad to worse at home. Karen suffered from depression and often called me at work to ask me to come home. I'd grown resentful of her neediness and was tired of missing work to attend to her every need. Was there any hope left for us?

When I returned from my trip, Karen continued to be unresponsive and depressed. I came home from work one day to find her stretched out on the couch with an icepack on her forehead. "These stupid meds aren't helping my migraines at all," she moaned. "I think they're just getting worse."

"I'm sorry," I mumbled half-heartedly as I shuffled past her toward the kitchen. "Hope you feel better." I took a deep breath, trying not to let my bitterness get the best of me. Why should I give up everything for a woman who had betrayed me? I couldn't be her savior; couldn't she see that?

In 1990, I befriended a teacher at the school where I worked as a speech pathologist. She shared with me one day that she had just gone through a painful divorce. I tried to comfort her and was flattered by how responsive she was toward my gestures. *Now here's a woman who really appreciates me,* I thought to myself.

Susan and I continued our friendship, and I grew to like her more and more. She was physically attractive, but more importantly, she liked me for who I was. When I cracked a joke, she laughed as if it was the funniest thing in the world. And when I smiled, she smiled back. Unlike Karen's eyes these days, hers were filled with life and warmth.

Two years after we started our friendship, I gave into my feelings and had an affair with Susan. I knew in my heart it was wrong, but I was swept away by her affection and admiration. I told myself I deserved to be happy and respected as a man. If my own wife could not make me feel this way, I'd have to find it elsewhere.

"I know it's crazy, but I want to be with you, Scott. Just leave Karen, and move near me," Susan suggested one night.

My head screamed, "No, don't do it!" but my heart screamed, "Yes, go for it!" I loved my children dearly and knew they wouldn't be happy with my decision, but perhaps they would understand one day. I broke the news to Karen one afternoon, explaining as calmly as I could that our marriage seemed beyond repair and that I needed to move on with my life.

"How could you think about leaving us like this?" Karen cried. "I've told you over and over I'm sorry! I don't know what else I could do!"

"It's not just the affair, Karen," I told her with a sigh. "It's more complicated than that. Susan and I … we belong together. You and I were too young. It was probably a mistake from the beginning. I'm sorry, but I hope you'll understand one day."

Tears streamed down Karen's face. "What about the kids? You think they will ever understand and forgive you?" she cried.

I shook my head, trying to keep my composure. "One day, I hope they will."

My heart and head continued to play tug-of-war as I packed my things and prepared to rent a room from an elderly woman near Susan's place. Deep down, I knew adultery was wrong, that even though Karen had been unfaithful, her actions didn't make mine acceptable. I knew divorce broke God's heart, and I was supposed to be a man of God. I taught a Bible study in my home, for goodness' sake! I was respected in the church, a man who was supposed to lead his family and encourage others to know God more.

Yet, they did not see what transpired behind closed doors, the pain I'd endured after years of turmoil with Karen. If they truly knew, they'd understand why I needed to leave. They'd want me to be happy, too.

About a year and a half later, in 1994, Susan and I married. Susan had three children of her own, and I tried my best to build a relationship with them. We began attending church together, and though I attempted to convince myself our life was good, the guilt over what I'd done still gnawed at me. My children were angry with me and made it very clear that they disapproved of my new marriage.

"So what do you guys want to do this weekend?" I asked when they came to visit during the holidays.

My daughter, now 15, just rolled her eyes. "Seriously, Dad? Enough with the games, pretending like we're this big happy family when we all know we're not. Mom's at home crying her eyes out, and you don't even care. What were you thinking?"

Her words cut to the core, and I cringed. "I'm sorry, sweetie. I love you guys so much, both of you. Sometimes when you get older, well, life gets really complicated. You'll see someday. What's happened between your mom and me doesn't change the way I feel about you and your brother."

"Yeah, that's what they all say," she mumbled, walking away.

My heart sank. Would my kids ever forgive me? Would we ever have a normal life again? *What have I done?* I wondered sadly, shaking my head.

In 2004, I discovered Susan was having an affair with a younger man she'd met on the Internet. I was devastated; how could I have trusted another woman, only to have her do the very thing I feared the most?

"I'm sorry, Scott … it just happened," Susan confessed. "Why don't we go to counseling? I really want to see our marriage work."

It just happened. Wasn't that the very thing Karen had said? Come to think of it, wasn't that the very thing *I'd* said when I left her? I was beginning to see the chain of destruction as we traded our hearts to another, leaving behind an aftermath of hurt, sadness and confusion. Could things ever be put back together again, or was it simply too late?

Susan and I visited different counselors, and after a while, I discontinued my sessions. Though we agreed to try to stay together and work things out, I grew controlling of her every move. If she got home a minute past 5 p.m., I assumed she'd been out fooling around. And if she was on the computer and had the screen turned away from me, I immediately grew suspicious that she was chatting with another man.

"Who are you talking to?" I asked, hovering over her chair.

"My friend," she snapped. "Leave me alone, Scott! I thought we agreed you were going to trust me!"

In 2005, Susan and I bought a large beautiful home in Visalia and hoped that perhaps a new place to live would bring a fresh start to our marriage. But months after we moved in, Susan announced she wanted a separation. She moved out, and I stayed in the home. The following year, we officially divorced.

I hit a new low that year, reeling from the pain of two failed marriages. I'd truly loved both Susan and Karen with all my heart; how could this have happened? What was wrong with me? I tried to move on with my life, but the betrayal haunted me day and night. I truly did love God and wanted to do what was right. I'd read my Bible and memorized verse after verse, I'd attended church nearly every week and I'd prayed with what I believed was a sincere heart. I knew I'd made my own share of mistakes, but I could not believe things had spun so terribly out of control. What was I still missing? And could I ever pick up the pieces and put my life back together again?

Desperate for a fresh start, I decided to check out a new church the following year. I sat near the back of the church each week as the pastor shared from the Bible. *I believe the Bible is true, God,* I prayed from my seat. *I want to serve you. But why does my life still feel like such a mess?*

At work, in the spring of 2009, I met the most beautiful woman I'd ever laid eyes on. Some time later, I finally asked her out for coffee. Little did I know, she had prayed that the man God wanted her to marry would specifically ask her out for coffee! So, of course, she accepted!

As we talked, Jeralyn shared about her relationship with Jesus. She spoke about him in a way I'd never heard any woman talk before, and she exuded an indescribable peace.

"I was in a hurtful relationship and finally got out," Jeralyn explained. "I was very wounded, but God helped me through all of it and brought a true healing in my heart. I am now filled daily with peace and joy because I know that God is the only one who can fill the emptiness in my soul. I realize that a relationship with him is something so much deeper than just memorizing Bible verses or even attending church; it's really knowing him for myself, just like a best friend."

That's what I want, I thought as she spoke. *That's what I've always wanted.*

"I go to this wonderful church called Bethel Family Worship Center in Tulare," Jeralyn went on. "It's like no other church I've ever attended. The people are so real and so welcoming, and the pastor always teaches a great message of truth and love. You should come with me sometime."

"I'd love to," I said eagerly.

Within just a couple months, I knew in my heart I

wanted to marry Jeralyn. I was very attracted to her, but it wasn't just her lovely figure, beautiful smile and stunning auburn hair that I found appealing. It was her beautiful heart that drew me in, and I knew that beauty came from her passionate love for God. Jeralyn was the sort of woman I'd been looking for my whole life.

Jeralyn and I married in Santa Barbara on October 3, 2009, and I knew I'd found a partner for life. We attended Bethel Family Worship Center together regularly, and I quickly saw why Jeralyn loved the church so much. The people became like family in no time, welcoming me with open arms. They all exuded the same joy Jeralyn did, and I soon realized just how contagious it was. Unlike my Catholic church, this one was not filled with rituals. Instead, it encouraged an authentic relationship with God. For the first time, I experienced a true, meaningful and powerful relationship with him.

My prayers were no longer desperate pleas for help, but prayers of thankfulness and adoration for all God had done in my life. The cycle of broken relationships was a result of the pain I'd endured in my past. But as I understood God's unconditional love for me, I was able to forgive myself and break the chains that had weighed me down for so long. I was truly a changed man.

In January 2010, I began experiencing complications with my health. Thinking I had a gallstone, I went to see a doctor. He performed a CT scan to rule everything out, and on January 10, he called me into his office with some shocking news.

"We've found a mass on your pancreas," he said grimly.

"A mass, as in … *cancer*?" The word stuck in my throat. How could that be?

"I'm afraid so. We need to run some more tests and put together a treatment plan right away."

I reeled at the news for days, gripped with fear and anxiety. "Pancreatic cancer is one of the worst to get," I told Jeralyn with despair. "The odds are bad … really bad."

"God is bigger than this," she encouraged me, taking my hand. "It's times like these we just want to give up, but this is when we need to press into God the most and surrender to him. He has mapped out your life since the beginning. We will pray for his healing and help to trust him."

I leaned into my wife, letting her hold me as the news sank in. I was so grateful for her strong faith; it would be so easy to succumb to my fear right now. Jeralyn was right; we had God on our side, and we would choose to trust in him.

Jeralyn continued our morning devotions together, focusing specifically on the book of Psalms in the Bible. The writer of the Psalms, David, had found himself in terrible trouble and had cried out to God for deliverance. Psalm 23:1-4 comforted me greatly in the same way I imagined it comforted David: "The Lord is my shepherd, I lack nothing. He makes me lie down in green pastures, he leads me beside quiet waters, he refreshes my soul … even though I walk through the darkest valley ... you are with me." I was about to walk through a dark valley, but I would not walk it alone.

The doctors placed a bilinary stent into my bile ducts, and a month later, we went to UCLA, where surgeons attempted to perform what they called a Whipple procedure to remove the tumor from my pancreas. When I awoke from surgery, they announced they were not able to remove all of the tumor as it was wrapped around a major artery connected to my liver.

"So we just went ahead and removed your gallbladder for now," the doctor said. "The best bet at this point is the traditional chemotherapy route. Since this is a very rare form of pancreatic cancer, I am referring you to a specialist."

Everything was happening so quickly. I'd gone from a healthy, vibrant man to a very sick patient under a microscope nearly overnight. The medical jargon flew around me, words I'd never thought I'd need to know. "God, help me be strong," I prayed. "You are my strength."

The following month, I began chemotherapy under the care of a well-known oncologist at UCLA who specialized in pancreatic cancer. He discovered a second tumor and prescribed a drug called Avastin, which he believed would drastically improve my chances of beating the cancer.

"So what are my odds, anyway?" I asked the doctor, bracing myself for the worst.

"Fifty percent," he said quietly.

I sat still in my seat, trying to breathe, but feeling my throat tighten as his words sank in. This meant there was a 50 percent chance I could live, but it also meant there was a 50 percent chance I could die. I was in my early 60s; the last third of my life was supposed to be filled with grandkids, golf, travel and relaxation. I still had too much living to do. I was not ready to die. I resolved to fight this thing with every ounce of my being and trust in God all the way through.

For the next year, Jeralyn and I made the three-hour trek to UCLA three times a month for my chemotherapy treatment. The chemo soon took a toll on my body. I lost 20 pounds, watched my hair fall out in chunks and endured painful sores in my mouth, as well as severe fatigue. I kept up my job, but the physical pain often made it difficult to effectively work all day. I had heard stories about the side effects of chemo, but I'd never been able to grasp just how horrific they were. It was as if my entire body was being ravaged by a horrid monster, and I could do nothing to stop it.

"The Lord sustains them at their sickbed and restores them from their bed of illness," Jeralyn read to me from Psalm 41 when I was too weak to read.

I clung to the words as I lay in bed, writhing in pain. I'd lost significant muscle mass so that doing simple things, like picking up a book, felt like I was lifting a 100-pound weight. I longed for the days when I could walk the golf course again, then wondered if I'd ever experience life as a normal person someday. *Fifty percent,* the doctor had said. What if there was no "someday"?

New side effects continued to emerge. Often, after a round of chemo, I vomited until it felt like my entire insides had come out. As my cell count plummeted, I contracted serious infections and wound up back in the hospital. Neuropathy kicked in, affecting my nerves and causing tingling and numbness. Jeralyn remained by my side, faithful, encouraging and strong.

While the cancer took a physical toll on my body, a new serious problem arose. The drug Avastin my doctor had been prescribing me was not FDA approved for the treatment of pancreatic cancer, and because of this, my insurance company refused to pay for it. Each treatment cost me $2,400 out of pocket, and the bill was getting steep.

My wife and I went to our friends at church, asking them to pray with us that God would resolve this issue. It seemed ironic and unfair to go into debt as I fought to stay alive. I knew God was in control, but as the bills piled up, I grew anxious. Would God come through for us? He said in his word we could trust him to provide, but this issue seemed so monumental, I could not imagine how it would be resolved.

"I'm put in a tough spot from an ethical standpoint," my oncologist told me with a sigh. "I don't want to stop treating you with this drug because it's working so well, and if I can be frank, I believe it's keeping you alive. You have one of the rarest cases of pancreatic cancer I've seen in all my years at UCLA. But I don't know how I can keep prescribing a drug I know isn't FDA approved."

We continued to pray, trusting in God to settle this growing issue. I wrote letters to the insurance company, explaining that the drug was helping me significantly and that I needed it in order to stay alive. But my appeals were repeatedly denied, and the bills continued to mount. We reached out to everyone we knew, from co-workers to family members, asking him or her to pray with us. It comforted me to know so many were praying.

One day, my co-worker came to me with a huge grin on his face. "Do you believe in divine intervention?" he asked.

"Of course," I replied, nodding. "Why?"

"Well, you're never going to believe this, but I was flying back to the West Coast this past week and was talking with a doctor next to me about how difficult it is to get payment for rare drugs these days," he began. "This other guy was sleeping near us, and when he woke up, he asked what we were talking about. We told him, and he explained that he used to be a representative for the drug Avastin! He gave me some suggestions for an appeal letter we could write, and I really think you could have a good chance at getting these bills paid!"

My jaw dropped at his words. "Wow, that's incredible! Definitely God!" I'd been praying and praying for answers, and at last, I had some hope.

My co-worker helped arrange a meeting with the regional representative for my insurance company. I prayed earnestly for God's direction in writing the appeal. "Let my words be the right words," I prayed. "Let them be the very ones that will convince these people to approve my drug." I thanked God for this huge breakthrough and prayed that it would be just what we needed to resolve everything.

In the letter, I carefully explained that the drug Avastin had been truly lifesaving for me. "Some doctors say I would have died 14 months ago without it," I wrote. "But I am still here today because it has worked." I explained in detail about my different CT scan results and how the tumors had significantly shrunk after treatment.

"The rest is in your hands, God," I whispered as I sent the letter off.

In September 2011, the appeal was granted, and the insurance company finally agreed to pay the now $44,000 in bills I'd racked up, as well as any future infusions of the drug. My wife, church friends, co-workers, family members and I all praised God for making what felt like the impossible become possible. He was, as Jeralyn continually reminded me, bigger than all of this.

☞☞☞

"When you're done watching the game, you want to head out for a walk?" Jeralyn called out to me from the kitchen.

"Yup, sounds great," I called back, turning my eyes back to the last few minutes of the basketball game. I loved watching my sports on TV, but I loved spending time with my wife even more. Always physically active, Jeralyn kept me on my toes.

While most people only endured chemotherapy for six months, I was now in my third year of treatment. I had not been declared officially cancer free, but I was still alive and able to do much of what I once could. Though my affliction had at times seemed too much to bear, I could now see how God was working all things together for good. He had drawn me closer to him through my suffering, and I'd been able to encourage many people who had walked down the same difficult road. The trivial things in life hardly seemed important anymore in light of the bigger picture. I believed the words in Psalm 41 that said God would "restore me from my bed of illness."

Whether God chose to fully heal me in this life or in heaven, I would someday spend eternity in his presence, complete with a new and perfect body. There would be no more chemotherapy pills, no more sores, no more pain. I would be made completely new.

As I flipped off the TV and went in search of my walking shoes, my journey over the past few decades played out in my mind. I'd spent so much of my earlier years struggling with issues of abandonment, fear and rejection. I'd then gone on to try to control my life in whatever way I could, but that hadn't truly helped ease the pain deep inside. After beginning a relationship with Jesus, I'd been a faithful Bible study leader, but merely doing good things hadn't truly transformed my heart. It was only after meeting Jeralyn and attending Bethel Family Worship Center that I'd fully understood that God simply wanted one thing: my heart. Only then did I really understand that God gave me chance after chance because he loved me so much. And only then was I set completely free from the pain of my past, and only then was I completely set free.

As the cancer ravaged my body, I was forced to give up all control — to surrender my entire being to God. Some nights, as I'd thrashed in pain in bed, I'd wondered what it was all for, how God could possibly receive praise from something so terrible. But he had sustained me, and through my trials, I'd seen his amazing provision and healing. My journey was not over, but I was confident that no matter what came my way, God would not abandon me.

"Let's go!" I called out to Jeralyn, glancing outside at the sun streaming through the window. It was a perfect California day for a walk, one that could not be passed up. Outside, with the trees in full bloom and the air perfectly crisp, life awaited. And I was ready for it. I was ready to live.

No Longer Alone
The Story of Mandy
Written by Angela Prusia

My sneakers squeaked against the gym floor and the volleyball stung my fist as I served the ball over the net. Finding my grandfather parked outside the school after practice surprised me.

"Where's Mom?" I asked, but he didn't answer.

I chattered about ordinary things, oblivious to what awaited. Favorite teachers. Friends. My freshman classes.

We turned onto our block, and the flashing lights made me straighten in my seat. *Why were the police at our home? Had there been an accident?*

I rushed inside, mentally tallying heads. Mom talked to an officer who took notes. My sister Karen hugged our grandmother, tears streaking their faces. *Where was Dad?*

Car wreck, I assumed. *He'd been hurt driving the dump truck.* His excavating job came with risk. I wasn't prepared for what hit me next.

"Mandy." A faceless person said my name. I only saw lips moving. Words hit my ears, but made no sense.

"Someone shot your father in the head."

Silent screams racked my body in protest.

The voice wouldn't stop lying. "Someone driving down the wooded road noticed the open truck door and found your father. Dead."

I wanted to block my ears. Claw at my flesh. Wake up from the nightmare.

"Your father left sometime mid-morning to get an excavating bid outside town. The call for help came a few hours later."

Unanswered questions stuck in my throat. *Why? Who did my dad meet? How come I didn't feel a jolt when the shot rang out?*

Tears spilled down my face.

Did my dad know how much I loved him?

Silence answered.

My father was gone.

Murdered in cold blood.

❧❧❧

The framed photo captured the smile I loved, but I couldn't bear to look. It rested in front of my father's closed casket. Seeing his face brought waves of grief, which threatened to undo me, so I stared at my patent leather shoes. Beside me, my grandparents cried. My mom clung to my sister, her face death white.

I couldn't remember how I got to the funeral. Or why I sat in the front row listening to a man talk about my father in the past tense. I pinched my flesh, sure this new reality was not my life. My dad couldn't be dead.

Outside, the sun blinded me. The flashing lights on the patrol car waiting to escort the funeral procession made me shudder. *How many days had passed since the police delivered the news of my father's murder?* I blinked at the line of vehicles waiting to follow us to the cemetery. I closed the door, wishing I could shut out the gaping faces.

Freshly churned dirt knotted my stomach. Dry heaves made me want to retch. The casket looked so cold. The man spoke again, but the words didn't stick. I stood over the gaping hole and clutched my chest. Emptiness swallowed me.

☙☙☙

Maybe my early teen years passed in relative ease because my father chose me. I adored him. And he loved me and my older sister like his own kids.

"I'd like to adopt you, Mandy," he surprised me one day during my sixth-grade year.

"Really?" I squealed in excitement. Ever since he and my mom quit drinking the previous year, boxes of Pepsi replaced the alcohol in our house. I couldn't have been happier — until now when he would officially become my dad.

"If you want this, you have to ask your father." My mom popped my bubble. Fear tainted my joy. *What would he say? How would he react?*

My birth father and I hardly talked. Our biweekly visits stopped when he remarried and plans to get custody of me fell through. After one particular hurtful visit, I couldn't face him anymore. Like my sister Karen had chosen months before, I stopped visiting.

"Tell your dad he doesn't have to pay child support anymore," my mom coached me. I didn't really understand what she meant, but I followed her lead.

I dialed the number. "Hi there." My voice caught. I no longer referred to my birth father as "Dad," so the undercurrent of awkwardness strained our conversation.

The surprise in his voice brought a twinge of guilt. Binge drinking and bitter fighting between my parents filled my earliest memories, but the aftermath always brought smiles. Sundays meant snuggling with my birth father on the couch, watching games of football or baseball. Reconciliation came in the form of ice cream or popsicles Mom and Karen brought back from grocery shopping. The day he set me on the washing machine to tell me about the divorce, I cried my eyes out.

"Are you sure this is what you want?" His voice through the phone scattered my thoughts.

"Yes," I answered, believing that's what I wanted.

Years later, after the murder, I saw how my mom and new dad manipulated me with the purchase of my beloved Shetland pony Sunshine. But for some reason, I never blamed him. *After all, wasn't the man who adopted me a saint?* My anger instead turned on my mother.

᭰᭰᭰

Old habits can return like friends, and Mom picked up the bottle again after losing my dad. With my sister married, the house cast long shadows on Mom's grief.

Rather than stay home alone with me, Mom dropped me off after sports practices and headed to the bar.

Alone and dying inside, I refused to get hurt again. Anger, bitterness and hatred took residence in the hole left in my heart. Mom — and later, her new boyfriend — became my favorite targets. I took pride in belittling them while sarcasm and obscenities spewed from my mouth.

"We're getting married," Mom announced my junior year.

"Don't expect any presents," I hissed, furious that she would even consider another man after my dad. "I'm not going."

The argument escalated, but neither of us backed down. She remarried, and I kept my word. I didn't attend the wedding.

❧❧❧

I buried my pain in high school sports and friends. During my senior year, I cheered along with the rest of the Bulldog fans at the opening game of the football season. Band music swirled through the air, mixing with the smells of popcorn and hotdogs from the concession stands. The game promised excitement, drawing most of the town of Belfair, Washington.

"Go, fight, win!" I stomped in the stands, feeling the metal bleachers reverberate underneath me.

"Is Brian excited for his senior year?" one of my friends asked me.

I eyed a certain running back on the field, the boyfriend I'd dated since my sophomore year.

"Are you kidding me? That's all he talked about this summer."

Suddenly the crowd rose. Groans peppered the stands.

"What happened?" I gasped. "Did Brian get hurt?"

She nodded. "It looked like the pass went one way and his leg bent the other direction."

I grimaced as the EMTs ran onto the field. *It's nothing,* I told myself, but the opposite soon proved true.

Puffy red eyes met mine when I visited Brian at his house the next day.

"Come in," his mom said, welcoming me. Pillows on the couch propped up his leg, which was fitted with a cast. His normally bright face looked pale.

"I'm so sorry." I rushed to hug Brian. "Are you in pain?"

Tears leaked from his eyes, something I'd never seen.

"I'm done." Devastation underscored his voice. "The doctor said I can't play the rest of the season. I've lost any chance of a scholarship."

I tried to argue, but my attempt fell short, so I sat next to Brian and wrapped my arms around him. I felt so helpless. "I'm so sorry," I whispered. "I'm so sorry."

❧❧❧

"Wanna come to church with me?" Brian asked a few days later. He hobbled down the halls at school on crutches. Around us, kids slammed lockers and hurried to class.

The question took me off guard. Brian and his family never attended church. "Church? Why?"

"I don't know." He shrugged. "I just want to go. I've been feeling like God wants me to do something different with my life."

I didn't know what to say. Even though we'd had our ups and downs in three years of dating, I'd always admired Brian's strong convictions as an athlete. He guarded his body by refusing to smoke or eat unhealthy foods and got upset when I made poor choices. The church thing was different, but seeing Brian handle his disappointment gave me new respect for him. He refused to let his injury crush him, despite the roadblock it erected in his path.

Going to church with Brian beat staying in an empty house, so I agreed. With Mom remarried, she and her husband often stayed weekends at his home in Oregon, a couple hours away. While I appreciated the space, the quiet reminded me how much I missed my dad and the time I called "the happy years." My own pain blinded me to my mother's hurt, and our lack of communication cemented a wall between us. Rather than let down my tough-girl act, I tore down my mom, driving her further away.

Unfortunately my rebellious reputation preceded me, so kids in the youth group didn't exactly welcome me when I tagged along with Brian. As a result, church became a turn-off. The situation at home determined my sporadic attendance on Sundays and Wednesdays. I shrugged off church on the good days; on the bad, I stomached church because it meant time with Brian. I didn't understand what he meant when he said he "surrendered" his life to Jesus, but it didn't matter. I couldn't wait to graduate.

❧❧❧

Soon after graduation, I enrolled in beauty school and moved an hour away to Kent, Washington. Brian's brother and sister-in-law opened their apartment to me, so I lived with them. Brian took classes at the community college in Kent as well.

Life away from home felt no different than the long nights and weekends I spent alone in high school. While the new city meant new friends and new parties, nothing erased the emptiness I felt since my dad's murder. His absence left me vulnerable and alone. My mom's escape to the bar had only heightened my isolation.

Immaturity and youth contributed to my on-again, off-again relationship with Brian. After a semester at the community college, he returned home to work at the nursery he'd worked at the previous summer. I finished my classes and returned home to take my state board exam and get a job at a hair salon.

Brian seemed different, but I didn't understand the change. He frequently talked about God or passages he'd read in the Bible.

"I've decided to put Jesus first in my life again," he told me when we got back together after our latest breakup. "I've made some mistakes, but the answer I found in high school is real."

I had no idea what he meant, but I started going to church with him again. The high school kids who turned me off still hadn't grown up, but Brian's best friend, Jake, and his mom, Millie, welcomed me every Sunday. Their acceptance and love softened me and changed my perception of the church and got me thinking about God.

Something inside me stirred when I heard the pastor talk about things from the Bible. The verses he shared touched me in a way nothing else had, answering my deepest feelings of loneliness.

Why not God?

I responded one Sunday when the pastor asked if anyone wanted to put his or her faith in Jesus. *So this is what Brian had been talking about all along.*

I walked up to the front of the church, continuing my inner dialogue. *Life's pretty crappy on my own. I might as well try you, Jesus.*

やややや

My foul mouth got an immediate cleaning, making others take notice. Circumstances at home didn't change, but I no longer felt alone. I learned the Bible verse, Ephesians 4:29, "Do not let any unwholesome talk come out of your mouths, but only what is helpful for building others up according to their needs, that it may benefit those who listen." It made me realize how destructive my words could be, so I began to talk differently to my mother.

Brian got excited about the changes and confided that he wanted to be a youth pastor. "When I first became a Christian, I didn't have a lot of good role models to encourage me. I want to help teens see how God can help them in their everyday lives."

For the first time, I understood.

আৰ আৰ আৰ

Soon after this, Brian, his oldest brother, his brother's girlfriend and I hung out in his brother's room one afternoon.

"Wanna get married?" Brian asked.

Everyone got quiet.

"Sure." I shrugged. He didn't have a ring, so I didn't think he was serious.

"Really?" He straightened, and I saw the sincerity in his eyes.

His brother and girlfriend stared at me, making my face go red. "Yeah, really."

Brian whooped, and my insides turned mushy. Brian wanted to spend his life with me.

Six months later, I walked down the aisle in the same church where I learned I didn't have to go through life empty and alone.

No Longer Alone

As Brian began his Bible classes and discussing topics with me, I realized how little I knew. A new desire to read the Bible helped me understand becoming a Christian was a journey rather than a destination. Some lessons came quickly; others took more sweat.

Three years after becoming a Christian, a huge roadblock loomed in my path.

If you do not forgive others their sins, your Father will not forgive your sins.

These words in Matthew 6:15 stopped me cold.

You need to forgive your mom, Jesus whispered deep inside me.

I started to argue until I remembered the many offenses he'd wiped off my slate.

If you do not forgive others their sins, your Father will not forgive your sins.

I read the words again. Forgiving would not be easy. But it was time to let go of the anger and the bitterness. Holding bitterness in my heart came with too steep a price.

జ్ఞ్ఞ్ఞ్ఞ్

"Can you forgive me?"

I imagined the awkward conversation during the hour-long drive to my mom's house. Nervous energy knotted my stomach.

Behind me, our new daughter, Jaqueline, slept in her

car seat. Life as a new mom held fresh promise. It seemed to be a glimpse of God's own parental love for me.

"I'm not expecting much." I talked to Jesus like he sat next to me.

That's okay, he seemed to answer in my heart. *This isn't about them.*

I nodded. Following Jesus was like falling in love, and I didn't want anything to stand in the way of us getting closer. Love came with sacrifices — in this case, kicking my pride out of the way and asking my mom and her husband to forgive me.

"Here we are, Jaqueline." I pulled up to the house and took a deep breath.

Mom met me at the door and helped me with her new granddaughter. We spent the afternoon catching up and playing darts in the garage she and my stepdad converted to a family room. After I put Jaqueline down for the night, I found them in the kitchen.

"I need to ask your forgiveness," I said. "I've been awful to you both over the years. And I'm sorry. I responded out of my hurt."

My mom eyed me, and I could see the regret reflected in her pupils. "I know." It was obvious she felt bad for her part, but she said nothing.

"Yeah," my stepdad piped up. "I thought you were a b****."

I exhaled. "You're right. I was."

The awkward silence I imagined descended, so I excused myself for bed. "See you tomorrow."

I walked away, feeling lighter than I had since my father's murder 10 years earlier.

ॐॐॐ

The next five years blurred together with the birth of two more daughters. Soon after our youngest turned 1, we packed our belongings and moved from Renton, Washington, to Tulare, California, where Brian would become a youth pastor.

The move brought both excitement and anxiety. Born and raised in Washington, neither of us had moved more than an hour from home.

Strangely enough, around the same time, my mom and stepdad moved to Michigan to help his special needs sister after his mother passed away, and Brian's parents moved home to Missouri.

Change was in the air. Still, leaving behind siblings and friends tugged at my heartstrings and tested me in ways I couldn't foresee.

For one, reality didn't quite match my expectations. I imagined my new life under palm trees at the beach. Instead I found myself in the middle of rural California. Waves of fruit and nut trees replaced my waves of blue water. Cows — not fish and other aquatic animals — populated the countryside. Rather than beach festivals, Tulare boasted a world-renowned farm show every February. To say I needed a mental adjustment was an understatement.

Another challenge came with daily life as a young mother of three not yet in school. In Washington, I had taken for granted play dates and bumping into friends at library reading time or grocery shopping. In Tulare, many days passed before I connected with other breathing adults.

I learned to rely on God as my friend even more. Unlike the long nights and weekends by myself in an empty house after my dad's murder, I felt God's presence with me. Even when the days revolved around one more mess to clean or another soiled diaper to change, Jesus was as close as my every breath.

He also blessed us with a great senior pastor and boss. Our new pastor and his wife immediately welcomed us — both to the church and to their immediate family. With our family more than 18 hours away and responsibilities at church during the holidays, travel wasn't an option. The pastor and his wife invited us to spend both Thanksgiving and Christmas with their family, and we instantly connected with their two sons, daughter, daughters-in-law, son-in-law and grandchildren. Being included in their family celebrations touched me deeply.

Our pastor also had an open door policy at work. Even when his office door was shut, no interruption was trivialized or ignored. He gave Brian the freedom to lead the youth as God directed him. This allowed Brian to concentrate on helping teens grow through connection in small groups. Since both Brian and I lacked strong mentoring in our early Christian years, this was especially close to his heart. Brian wants to see teens grow into adults passionate about their relationships with Jesus and committed to passing the torch to their children.

ॐॐॐ

People in Tulare who don't know my past are surprised I wasn't raised in a picture-perfect home. I, too, sometimes look in the mirror, amazed at the person Jesus is shaping me to be. I remember the lonely, angry, bitter girl whose world shattered the fatal day of her father's murder. And I remember the day I put my faith in Jesus, who changed that hurting girl into the woman I am today.

Life is full of unresolved issues and circumstances we can't control. My father's murder has never been solved; justice has yet to be served. But I've learned I don't have to walk alone through the pain life brings. Jesus will someday make everything right. But today, he wants to give me freedom. Forgiveness breaks the shackles of bitterness and anger. Jesus is waiting — if only we'll surrender.

A BEAUTIFUL TAPESTRY
The Story of Tari
Written by Karen Koczwara

"You will walk with a cane the rest of your life," the doctor said matter-of-factly. "Your balance will always be off, and you may never be able to drive again."

Walk with a cane the rest of your life. Never drive again. I sank into the chair and took in his words, gulping them down like a taste of bitter medicine. *Never* was such a final word; not quite a death sentence, still a devastating blow. I had plenty of life ahead, life that was supposed to be spent golfing and chasing my grandkids through the park on warm summer days. I was only 61 years old, and I had plans! And now those plans were dashed, my life changed forever in an instant.

"We'll check on your progress every six months," the doctor said, but his words sounded foreign and far away.

I nodded resignedly, but inside, something rose up in my chest like a roaring fire. *Hope.*

Hope that I would prove him wrong, against all odds, and be completely healed.

ॐॐॐ

I was born in 1937 in the little town of Clayton, New Mexico, on the border of Texas, Oklahoma and Colorado. With a population of just a few hundred people, Clayton is best known for its agriculture, trout fishing and rural appeal. It is also known as the "Crossroads Country," and it was here in this small town that my own life came to a crossroads one day.

My two older brothers, younger sister and I were raised by an adoptive mother and father. My adoptive mother had always loved children but had never been able to have any of her own. She made our home a wonderful place, filling our days with love, laughter and hot meals on the dinner table. I was a happy little girl, enjoyed school and had plenty of friends to explore the countryside with. My life seemed destined for, at the least, ordinary success.

And then one day, my mother did not look quite right. Her normally rosy cheeks were now pale, and she could hardly get out of bed. I had never seen my mother sick a day in my life, and concern rose inside. "You okay, Mama?" I asked in a small voice.

"Don't know what's come over me," she replied weakly.

We soon found out what had come over my mother — a baby! At 42 years old, my mother had finally conceived! She found a local doctor — who I guessed to be about 100 years old from his lined face and thinning hair — to deliver the baby when it came time. I watched in awe as her belly grew bigger each day and her dresses became so tight she could hardly move.

"When will it be time?" I asked with mounting excitement. At age 10, I had given up playing with dolls, but I looked forward to caring for a real baby now.

"Soon," she replied wearily. "I can tell it's going to be soon."

And then one day, it was time. My mother's pains grew so bad she let out shrieks, and she called her doctor with the news. He met her at the hospital, where she labored for hours and hours, until the sun sank into the ground and the little town shut down. At last, the doctor realized the baby wasn't coming out, and he performed a C-section. But it was too late. As the healthy little boy stretched his tiny arms into the world for the first time, my mother took her last breath.

My two older brothers went off to military service, leaving my father, my sister and me to raise a newborn on our own. We awkwardly diapered, fed and rocked him, all the while grieving a mother who gave up her life for another. Things quickly went from bad to worse at home. Though my father worked hard in the fields, the money soon ran out, and we lost our little house to the bank. We moved into a three-room shack, leaving behind life as we knew it down the road. The hot meals my mother had once made were replaced with whatever we could scrounge up; often, my tummy rumbled as I drifted off to sleep.

Not yet a teenager, I learned to grow up overnight, mothering that little baby as though he were my own. But as I rocked him back and forth, I often wondered about the mother who'd given me up to another.

Her wallet-sized photo sat in my bottom dresser drawer, and I sometimes pulled it out. *We had the same nose,* I thought, *and maybe the same chin.* Did she ever think of me?

My father found a woman to watch the baby while my sister and I went to school. For a few hours each day, I was an ordinary kid at a desk, working arithmetic problems and scribbling spelling words.

But the minute I got home, reality set in again. There was no food, the baby cried and my father was drinking again.

How could we go on like this?

When I was 13 years old, my grandfather showed up at our door. He had moved his family to Denver years before and sometimes returned to Clayton to visit his aging parents. As I tucked my siblings into bed, I heard him talking in hushed tones to my father in the other room.

"That girl is at an age where she needs a mother. I'd like to take her back to Denver to live with me and her grandmother."

I sucked in my breath. *He must mean me!* But who would take care of my siblings? How would they survive when my father drank away every last penny we had? My heart fluttered as I leaned against the wall, trying to hear the rest of their words.

The next day, my father asked me to pack my belongings and go with my grandfather to Denver. I obeyed, glancing back sadly at the little three-room shack that held all that was left of our crumbling lives. *Let my siblings be okay,* I prayed as I stepped into the car. *And please, God, let me be okay, too.*

I couldn't remember when I'd first started talking to God. He'd just sort of always been there, like a friend I'd known forever. My grandfather shared about him often, referring to him as a "loving God who cares for us." I believed it was true, even on the worst days when the milk ran out and the little shack grew dark and lonely. I had to believe, for there was nothing else to do.

My grandmother welcomed me into her home with a big hug, and as I fell asleep on my new bed that night, I wondered if I might be okay after all. I'd make new friends in Denver, get a fresh start, maybe even meet my first boyfriend here. But just a week later, my hopes were dashed once again.

"She's your daughter and your responsibility!" I heard my grandfather hiss into the phone. "I'm putting her on the first flight I can get to San Francisco, and you better be there to pick her up!"

I gulped, my heart racing wildly. There was only one person he could be talking to — my biological mother! A wave of mixed emotion overwhelmed me as I slipped back into my room. *This* was what he'd meant when he told my father I needed a mother? Why didn't he want me here? And how could I just go live with a mother I'd never met before? If she'd given me up the first time, why would she want me now?

The questions raced through my mind, toppling over one another as I packed my things the next morning. I stared out the window as the Colorado landscape whizzed by; I might never see it again. San Francisco seemed a world away. I'd always longed to see the ocean, and deep down, I'd always longed to see my mother, too, but how could I just slip into her life after all these years?

"This is for the best, kid," my grandfather said, hugging me as the plane pulled into the gate. "You're growing up now, and you need a mother in your life. You'll do just fine in California."

How can you be so sure? I wanted to cry, but instead, I held back the tears and bravely boarded the plane.

I sat tensely in my seat, watching as the Colorado sky disappeared into the clouds. At last, I drifted off, and when I woke up, the clouds were still there, this time hovering over a majestic red bridge. I'd heard about this bridge — the beautiful Golden Gate. We were in San Francisco, and I was about to meet my birth mother for the very first time.

So nice to meet you, I practiced under my breath as I debarked the plane. *No, it's a pleasure to meet you.* People in California practiced their manners, and I wanted to make a good first impression. *Pleasure to meet you, and thank you for coming for me. I'm sure we're going to have a lovely time.* No, that sounded too formal. *Just be yourself.*

My heart jumped in my chest as I saw her striding toward me — the woman I'd seen in the picture. She was pretty, with soft features and perfectly kempt hair. But she did not smile as she stopped in front of me, nor did she reach out for a hug. "Tari?"

"It's me," I said in a small voice.

Was I a disappointment? If only I'd had a chance to brush my hair before getting off the plane.

"Where'd you get that ugly ratty old coat you're wearing?" she huffed, rolling her eyes in disdain.

I stared at her in disbelief. "It's all I have," I replied softly.

"Hmph." She stepped back, still inspecting me. "Well, let's get going now, shall we?"

We rode in silence all the way home. I took it all in — the tall, stately buildings, the hilly roads, the bustling crowds and honking taxi cabs. *This is home now,* I told myself numbly. *And this is your mother driving the car, the woman who gave birth to you.* Yet why did it feel like I'd just been dumped in a strange land with a stranger who didn't like me already?

We finally reached the house; it was pleasant enough and a far cry from the three-room shack back in New Mexico. I gingerly stepped through the front door, and a little girl jumped off the couch with a smile.

"I have a surprise," my mother said to the little girl, motioning toward me. "We have a big sister for you."

The little girl stared up at me with her big, round eyes and then raced forward to hug me. I hugged her back, embracing her warmth. At last, someone wanted me! "Nice to meet you," I said when we finally pulled away. "We're going to have lots of fun."

❧❧❧

Senior year is an exciting time for most, filled with parties, prom and the anticipation of an exciting future ahead.

But mine would include none of those things, for I was moving away once again.

"We're getting a divorce," my mother explained. "It's hard to explain, but it's for the best. Pack your things, Tari. We're moving out of state next week."

My heart sank at her words. I glanced around the room I'd worked so hard to make my own. It had never quite felt like home here since I'd arrived. Though my younger sister adored me, my mother and stepfather had never fully accepted me as part of the family. I'd felt like an intruder since day one, a stranger looking inward. I'd watched with longing as my sister climbed on my parents' lap at night to watch TV, watched them cuddle happily together while I stood off to the side. *You never really wanted me, not then, and not now,* I'd told myself sadly over and over.

I'd lost all contact with my adoptive family; my world back in New Mexico seemed a lifetime ago. But I'd made a life for myself in San Francisco, made friends and even learned to like school. And things had been okay … until now. Now my world was turned upside down, and the timing could not have been worse.

"Where are we going to live?" I asked my mother as we piled into the car with the last of our belongings.

She shrugged. "We're heading east," she said vaguely. "We will figure it out."

East. The only thing I knew about my life right now was that it was headed east. I glanced back as the Golden Gate Bridge disappeared into the distance. I should have known better; nothing in my life stayed for good.

At last, we stopped in Salt Lake City, Utah, where my mother announced I'd be staying with her sister. "You'll be fine here, Tari," she said.

"And what about you?" I asked, dumbfounded.

"Your sister and I are going on to Denver for now. It's just for a little bit."

And just like that, there I was again, on the steps of a stranger's house with only a suitcase to my name. A teenage girl with the whole world ahead of her, yet it just felt like mine had ended.

I waded through my senior year of high school, hardly bothering to make new friends. What was the point, when they'd all grown up together, and I'd probably never see them again in a few months? Loneliness crept in, and I turned to the only friend I had — God. Despite feeling alone and rejected, I still believed he hadn't given up on me. I still believed he cared about the girl in the ratty old coat, the girl who'd never really belonged anywhere.

When graduation came along, my mother showed up, much to my surprise. "You're going back to Denver with me," she said matter-of-factly. "You can figure out the rest of your life there."

I'd invested nothing in Salt Lake City, so I had nothing to lose. Yet as we climbed into the car, I wondered if I'd ever settle down. Would I spend the rest of my life like this, following orders like a serviceman in the military? Or would I someday find a place to call home?

The summer was pleasant in Denver, unlike the scorching heat in New Mexico or the seemingly endless fog in San Francisco. "I'll get a summer job," I told my mother.

"No, you're going to business school," she insisted. "It's the only logical choice."

But I didn't want to go to business school. For once, I set my foot down. "I'm going to look for a job," I replied with all the confidence I could muster. "And I'm sure I'll find one."

I befriended my next-door neighbor, and she encouraged me to interview for a job as a credit checker at a local company where she worked. I did, and I landed the job right away. For the first time in years, a shred of hope surged through me. I'd gotten my first real job! I was going to succeed!

"I got the job, Mom!" I cried, flying through the door that afternoon. "I start right away."

My mother rolled her eyes. "That will never work out, Tari. But go ahead. Get it out of your system, and then you can do the sensible thing and go on to business school."

I quickly learned the ins and outs of my new job and soon moved up in the company, proving my mother wrong. I met a nice girl at work, and we discussed getting an apartment together. I took her home to meet my mother, and we shared our plans.

"You will never make it on your own out there," my

mother replied, quickly shooting down the idea. "Do you know how expensive things are? And with your little salary? Forget it. You're not getting your own place."

I'd thought my mother would be happy to have me independent and out of her hair, but instead, she seemed disappointed in me once again. Dejected, I gave up on the idea and focused on succeeding at my job.

One day, I happened upon a Navy recruiting office down the street. I stopped in. "Can women join the Navy, too?" I asked.

"Oh, yes, we have lots of programs for young women," the officer replied. "If you have a few moments, I can tell you all about it."

That afternoon, I returned home, hardly able to contain my excitement. "I signed up for the Navy!" I gushed to my mother. "I'm really doing it!"

"That's the stupidest thing I ever heard. Why would you go and do a thing like that?" My mother's eyes were fiery; I'd never seen her so furious.

"This is my life, and this is what I'm doing," I said firmly. "I've already made up my mind." I fingered the brochure the officer had given me; it depicted a life of adventure and promise. For once, I was making my own choices, and no one could talk me out of it.

I left for Basic Training in Bainbridge, Maryland, and graduated at the top of my class. From there, I went on to dental technician school and graduated at the top of my class there, too. My instructors explained that there were plenty of opportunities for my skills all around the country; it was up to me to choose where I wanted to go. The idea of having a say in where I lived excited me. I stared at a map, my eyes drifting to the state of Florida. I'd heard all about its sunny, warm beaches; they were nothing like the chilly San Francisco shores.

"I'll go to Pensacola, Florida," I decided.

Not long after I arrived in Florida, I laid eyes on the most handsome man I'd ever met. He was a dental technician in the military, too, and the minute our eyes locked, I thought to myself, *I'm going to marry this man. I just know it.*

"I'm Larry," the handsome man said, extending his hand.

I shook it, hoping he didn't notice my heart pounding inside my chest and the color creeping into my cheeks. "Tari. Nice to meet you."

Larry and I began dating, and within just a couple months, we began to discuss marriage. "I know we might seem crazy, and it's all been so quick, but I want to marry you," I told him eagerly.

"How about the day before Christmas? How perfect would that be?" Larry suggested.

"Yes!" I agreed. "We'll do it."

I called my mother, bracing myself for her usual disapproval. "I know you probably think we're rushing into this, but we're truly in love," I explained.

"I think it's impulsive," she said. I could almost see her rolling her eyes on the other end of the line.

"I know it seems that way, but I'd really like you to

think about helping us with arrangements. We don't have much time," I said.

"I'll think about it," she replied with a sigh.

Next, we called Larry's parents; they were both beside themselves. "You've barely just met that girl!" they said disapprovingly.

"I just want you to meet her. You'll love her as much as I do," Larry insisted.

We went to meet his parents in Denver, and to my disappointment, they did not welcome me with open arms. His mother was cordial but cold, inspecting me with a wary eye from across the dinner table. I tried to make pleasant conversation, but I could sense their reluctance.

Larry took his parents into the other room, and I overheard them discussing our future. "Look, I want to marry this girl. I'm in love with her."

"You're only 19," his father retorted. "You have to be 21 to marry without our consent."

"Yes, but I am in love," he said, keeping his composure.

"It will never work," said his mother, her voice rising.

"If you won't let us get married here, we will go to New Mexico, where they allow marriage without parental consent. You won't be there to see the ceremony, and you will regret it," Larry pressed.

At last, his parents relented. "All right, if this is what you want to do, I guess we can't talk you out of it."

December 24 was rapidly approaching, and we both realized we could not pull off a wedding before Christmas.

But a week later, on New Year's Day, Larry and I married in a simple but beautiful ceremony. I had no regrets about our quick courtship; I had known from the moment I met him that he was the man for me. The odds were against us, but I was convinced that with God by our side, we would find a way to make it.

There was no time for a honeymoon; we had to return to the base in Florida in two days. We spent the night in a motel and reported back to work the next day. When we returned, Larry learned he had orders to go to the West Coast. My heart sank. "We have to be together," I insisted. "They have to find a way to keep us together."

The Navy secured a place for me to live in San Diego, and I made the cross-country move again. By now, I had learned to accept a life of adventure and uncertainty. I was thankful that, despite all the unknowns the future held, God was the one certain in my life. I remembered the words of my grandfather when I was a child: "God will never leave or forsake you." My world had been rocked plenty of times, but I felt God had never abandoned me. No matter where I ended up, I knew somehow it was all going to be okay.

We settled into life in San Diego, with its wide beaches and year-round sunny skies. I began work as a dental technician at the Marine Recruitment Station; my job entailed removing the rotten teeth of the servicemen as they came into the office. It wasn't the most pleasant job, but it was one I'd practically learned to do in my sleep, and I enjoyed chatting with the men and learning their stories of travel around the world.

One warm March day, as I held the aspirator in a man's mouth, I suddenly grew very nauseous. Bile rose into my mouth, and I stepped back, fearing I might throw up. "I think I have the flu," I muttered to the captain beside me. "I need to go to the sick bay."

A visit to the sick bay confirmed I was pregnant. "Pregnant? Are you sure?" I could barely get the words out. Larry and I had only been married a couple months, and though we'd discussed having children, we'd been in no hurry to do so.

"I'm sure," the doctor replied. "It looks like you'll have to be discharged from the service."

Discharged. Just like that, my Navy career was over. I was going to be a mother!

I told Larry the news, and he hugged me. "We'll be okay. This is good news, Tari, remember?"

"I know," I said, trying to be excited. "I just ... what if I'm not a good mother?"

"You'll be the best," he insisted with a smile.

My own birth mother had never really accepted me, and the mother I'd known as a child was now only a distant memory of happy times. I was determined that I would shower this child with every ounce of love I had. Even if we did not have all the riches in the world, this child would know it was loved.

Larry's ship was dry-docked in San Francisco for repairs, so we moved there while they worked on it. I spent the remainder of my pregnancy there, watching my belly expand and the baby jump inside as it grew bigger and bigger. The Navy sent Larry out on weeklong assignments; he returned every Friday.

One Thursday when he was gone, I awoke early in the morning with terrible cramps. It took me a moment to realize what was happening — I was in labor!

I stumbled to a neighbor's house at 5 a.m., and she helped me to the hospital. Minutes after we arrived, I delivered a beautiful little baby girl. Larry arrived at the hospital a short time later, but the doctors did not allow him to come into the room until that afternoon.

"I'm so sorry I missed the delivery," Larry apologized. "Talk about crazy timing. Guess this little girl couldn't wait to meet her mother." He gripped our daughter's tiny finger, and we both stared at her for a while in awed silence.

Larry got news that he was shipping out to sea in two weeks just after we brought our daughter home. "I don't want you here by yourself," he insisted. "I'll see if you can stay with my parents while I'm away."

He called his parents, who agreed to let me and the baby live with them in Denver until Larry returned. "Are you sure this is such a good idea?" I asked. "I don't want to impose."

"Are you kidding? When they take one look at this little girl, they're going to fall in love with both of you," he replied, kissing me on the forehead.

I moved to Denver, where Larry's parents took me in, this time with open arms. They gave me a car so I could get around the city, and we got along beautifully. When the baby kept me up all night, Larry's mother took her so I could nap. And when I caught her rocking her new little granddaughter to sleep, my heart melted. This was my family now, a little piece of home.

Our daughter, Cyndy, was 10 months old when she and Larry were reunited. She was now a chubby, babbling little girl on the verge of taking her first steps. When Larry ran to give her a hug, she crumpled her little face and began to cry.

"It's going to take time," I assured him. "She doesn't know you yet. She'll grow to love you soon, you'll see."

And just as I'd promised, Cyndy and Larry formed a special bond in no time at all. My heart surged with happiness as I watched him scoop her into the air and fly her around the room. Less than two years ago, I'd been a naïve girl in Denver, ready for adventure when I signed up for the Navy on a whim. Now I had a family of my own: a husband who adored me and a perfect little girl I could hardly believe was mine. God had been so faithful, bringing me out of those dark, lonely times, giving me the future and hope the Bible talked about. Somehow I knew that, no matter what life threw our way, we were all going to be just fine. The adventure had just begun.

☙☙☙

After the birth of my daughter, the doctors told me I might never conceive again. I had cysts on my ovaries, which made it nearly impossible to get pregnant. But Larry and I continued to pray over the years, and when my daughter was 9, we overcame those doctor's odds and delivered a healthy little boy, Darren, into the world. When the doctors recommended a hysterectomy after his birth, I felt a peace about the procedure. God had been so good to bless us with a boy and a girl, and we were thankful for his abundant provision. Our family was now complete.

We lived in San Diego until Larry was discharged from the Navy, and for the next 32 years, we made our home in Hacienda Heights in Southern California. Larry and I raised our children there and both worked for a large bank for years. When it was taken over by Bank of America and we learned we could take early retirement, we decided to do just that. We looked forward to spending time with the grandkids someday, traveling a bit and, of course, golfing.

My daughter married, and she and her new husband had two little boys we adored. My son-in-law applied for a job as a correctional officer and completed his schooling in Galt, California. When he got a job, they relocated to nearby Tulare, a beautiful little town in the San Joaquin Valley. I was sad to see them go, and Larry and I discussed moving to be closer to their family.

"I can't stand not seeing those little boys," I said. "Why don't we go check out Tulare, and see if we can't move there ourselves?"

We did, and we soon fell in love with the little town, situated conveniently a couple hours from the mountains and the beach. We moved there and enjoyed being closer to our grandsons. My son, Darren, and his family followed as well. I was thrilled we were all in the same place. Life was good, and I was content. Except for one thing.

Since arriving in Tulare, we had tried out a few churches and at last settled on one nearby. I got involved in the choir and helped usher, but the church never quite felt like home. Many of the people had been there for years and didn't seem to welcome newcomers; I felt like I had back in San Francisco as a teen, an outsider looking in.

"You should check out our church," my daughter suggested one day. "Bethel Family Worship Center is really great. God is doing some amazing things there, and the people are so welcoming."

I mentioned it to Larry. "Maybe we should go check out Cyndy's church," I told him.

We went the next Sunday, and just as Cyndy promised, everyone welcomed us with open arms the minute we walked in the doors. As we sat through the service, I felt something I hadn't felt in years, if ever. It was like a warm coat on a chilly day, and though I couldn't quite put my finger on it, I knew we'd found a place to belong.

Larry and I enjoyed getting involved in the church, and as the weeks went by, something stirred inside of me. I felt like I had known God my whole life, but for the first time, I felt like I truly knew him as the intimate friend my grandfather often talked about. The beautiful worship time encouraged me to explore places in my heart I never had before, and the message challenged me not just to read my Bible more, but to really develop a true love and desire to know God. As I turned over the hurts of my past I'd buried for so long, I felt God bring me to a new place of healing.

I finally understood what they were explaining at our new church. They explained that the Bible says that God loved me so much that he didn't want to punish me — or anyone else — for the times we had hurt or been bitter toward others. So he let his son, Jesus, pay for our wrongdoings instead. They explained that the Bible says all I had to do was ask for God's forgiveness and believe in what Jesus did, and I could experience peace and strength as I unloaded my past to him.

And so, I gave every fear and every heartache over to God. The load was lighter. The sky seemed brighter. Life suddenly held fresh promise.

Both my new town and new church felt like the real home I'd never had.

෧෧෧

"Have a good day on the golf course!" I called out to Larry as he packed his clubs and headed out the door. "See you this afternoon!"

"Love you!" Larry called back as the door closed behind him.

I sat down at the kitchen table and picked up my crafts. I loved sitting in my cozy kitchen, the sun streaming through the window as I put my hands to work. Despite turning 61 that year, I hadn't slowed down a bit. Sometimes I joined Larry on the golf course for a round or two, but often I enjoyed the peace and quiet in the house, just me and God.

As my fingers wove the needle through the fabric, I thought about the last few decades of my life. Like my crafts, my life had often resembled a mess of scattered pieces in the beginning, but in the end, the result had been a beautiful work I could take pride in. Of course, God was the master weaver, the painter, the one who had fit all those scattered pieces together. I didn't know where I would be without his strength and guidance.

I picked up a needle with my right hand, and it suddenly dropped to the ground. I tried to reach down to grab it, but I couldn't. Baffled and a bit frightened, I slowly got up and shuffled over to the recliner, where I sat until Larry finally got home.

"I can't move my right side at all," I told Larry, panic rising in my chest as I tried to demonstrate. "I need you to take me to the emergency room right away."

Larry helped me to the car, and we sped off to the hospital, where the doctors admitted me and performed an MRI immediately. They returned with grim news. "You've had a stroke," they said. "We will run some more tests, but it looks like it was at the lowest part of the brainstem. This is the part of the brain that carries all the sensory messages to the body and tells it how, when and where to move."

My head spun a bit as the words sank in. *A stroke.* "Will I … be okay?" I asked. My voice didn't sound right to my own ears.

"Only time will tell the lasting effects," the doctor explained. "Most people end up learning to walk again with the help of a cane, and some fully regain their speech. Some don't. Each case is different."

Even in my confused and fatigued state of mind, I didn't like the sound of what he said. Larry and I had looked forward to years of active retirement. We had grandkids to chase and dreams to chase, too! I was too young to spend the rest of my life hobbling around with a cane.

Larry called the church right away so people could pray, and several of our friends came to visit. Once again, I was so grateful for Bethel Family Worship Center, where everyone had become like family. I couldn't imagine going through this alone.

Over the next few weeks, I learned the full extent of my condition. My stroke had affected everything from my speech to my memory to my body movement. My face now drooped on the right side, and I slurred my words when I spoke. My right leg had no feeling, and I could not even hold a pencil to write or lift anything heavy at all. When I did try to walk, I had difficulty balancing, and I had no depth perception, which made it hard to gauge how near or far things were nearby. Overnight, I had been transformed into a person I hardly recognized in the mirror.

The doctors released me with blood pressure medication and started me on physical and speech therapy. Over the next several months, I worked hard with the therapists to regain my speech and my movement, but I did not recover completely.

"This is the best we can do for you right now," the doctors eventually told me. "You will walk with a cane for the rest of your life."

Their words sounded final, but I chose to believe that my God was bigger than any medical diagnosis — that he could heal me completely if he wanted to. The pastors prayed over me for healing during the service each week.

"We believe you are able, God," they prayed. "Please touch and heal Tari's body from head to toe."

But God did not choose immediate healing. I kept up my faith, believing that he would heal me in his perfect timing. Some days, I grew discouraged as I watched my husband walk out the door to play golf or visit the grandkids. The DMV refused to renew my driver's license because of my depth perception issues; this forced me to have to rely on my husband and relatives for rides to the store, church and anywhere else I needed to go. While I was grateful for their unselfish help, I longed for the day when I could get behind the wheel again and regain my independence.

On the days that grew long, frustrating and lonely, I prayed and turned to my Bible to read God's words. One of my favorite verses was Isaiah 40:29-30: "He gives strength to the weary and increases the power of the weak.

Even youths grow tired and weary and young men stumble and fall. But those who hope in the Lord will renew their strength. They will soar on wings like eagles; they will run and not grow weary; they will walk and not be faint."

God was my hope and my strength. I would not grow weary in my conviction that he would heal me and that I would walk — even run — again someday.

I attended ladies' retreats with the church each year, and every time they offered prayer during a service, I accepted. Women prayed over me, asking for healing, but God didn't seem to be answering. "God, I give this up to you," I prayed repeatedly. "I do believe you will heal me, but in the meantime, I will trust in you and know that you are in control of all situations."

Larry remained a stable support, encouraging me all the way. "You're doing so well," he assured me. "Just think of how far you've come in your therapy."

"Someday I will give up that cane, though," I told him with a determined smile. "I know I will."

❧ ❧ ❧

In 2006, seven years after my stroke occurred, I went to yet another ladies' retreat. On Friday night, I met the speaker for the weekend, a pastor's wife from a nearby town. "I'll see you tomorrow afternoon," she said before we headed to bed.

The next afternoon, as I sat in the session, the speaker

took her place at the front and cleared her throat. "Ladies, God spoke to me and told me not to prepare what I had in mind for this evening's session. He said he would let me know at the proper time what he had planned. So be prepared to be surprised," she added with a smile.

That evening, I enjoyed the beautiful worship music, thanking God for letting me enjoy a wonderful time at the retreat and for letting me feel his presence. The speaker then took the stage and spoke again. "The Lord spoke to me and told me he wants me to do a healing. I believe there are several special women here who need healing."

My heart raced in my chest. *That's me, that's me!* I wanted to shout out. Instead, I stood calmly as everyone formed a circle and several women stepped out to pray. I raised my good hand up to heaven and prayed along with the women as they asked God to touch my body and heal me from my stroke.

Suddenly, I felt a warm sensation through my fingertips all the way down the right side of my body. At that moment, I knew I was healed! Seven years after my stroke, he answered my prayers.

I ran up to the front, hardly able to contain my excitement and joy. Everyone gazed at me in disbelief, expecting me to turn cartwheels like a little girl. I was healed! I was healed!

I called Larry after the session and blurted out the wonderful news.

"God healed me tonight!" I cried. "I can walk, I can move my arm, I can dance … and best of all, I don't need that ol' cane anymore! I can't wait to show you when I get home tomorrow!"

"Oh, Tari, that's wonderful!" he cried.

We both rejoiced in what God had done. As I hung up the phone, happy tears spilled down my cheeks, and I didn't bother to wipe them away.

I practiced a little dance, marveling at the way my limbs worked so well. It was as if nothing had ever happened. I was as good as new!

I could hardly fall asleep that night as I thanked God over and over for his amazing healing. I had never stopped believing that he could and would heal me, even when despair crept in and threatened to win. I had never given up hope, even when the doctors' words seemed so final. God had restored me and made me whole again from head to toe, and I would shout his goodness from the mountaintops for the rest of my life.

❧❧❧

"Mom, you are glowing," my daughter said, hugging me one afternoon not long after the retreat. "You're seriously glowing."

"You are," Larry agreed. "You have never looked more beautiful."

I laughed. "I feel beautiful. I may be 74, but I've now got the energy of a 20 year old! So watch out!" It felt so good to laugh. But it felt even better to be surrounded by my family, the ones who had stood by my side, prayed with me and believed along with me that God would heal me in his perfect timing.

I got my driver's license back and started work at a temp job that required me to stand on my feet for long periods of time. "No problem," I told my new employer. "I can do it." I honestly believed that when God had healed me, he'd added in an extra dose of super energy for good measure. I was certain I could now walk those 18 holes on the golf course with Larry — no problem.

I picked up my crafts one afternoon and began to work. It had been a long time since I'd been able to sew with such ease, and it felt good to see a project come to completion at last. My life had been a tapestry of wounds, trials, beauty, uncertainty, loneliness, joy and healing, but in the end, my journey would result in a beautiful masterpiece, handcrafted by God. The pieces would all be sewn together, each bearing a unique purpose in the final result. And it would be good. Only in heaven would I see the beautiful result of my story on earth. But for now, I was walking free in the hope and joy that only came from him.

Twice Adopted
The Story of Travis
Written by Joy Steiner Moore

I pushed the pedal to the floorboard around the bend in the two-lane California road. Hands locked tight on the steering wheel, I whizzed past a telephone pole on my right, then a big pickup truck in the opposite lane, then another telephone pole.

With its narrow curves around flower-covered foothills, the road was known for dangerous blind spots. Signs posted every few miles read, "Stay Alive on Highway 65."

It would be so easy, I thought. *It would look like an accident.*

Accidents happened all the time here. I drove this route every day for my job as a courier, and I had seen many close calls. In fact, I had come up on a fatal collision just a couple of weeks ago.

I loosened my grip on the steering wheel and stared at another telephone pole coming up on my right. In my mind's eye, I pictured my red two-door hatchback crashing headfirst into the post, wrapping itself into a mess of twisted metal. I imagined my funeral at our tiny church: my stepdad, John, bravely leading the service through his tears and Susan grieving on the front row — that is, if she even bothered to come. I saw instant relief and peace for myself — an escape from a life that was quickly unraveling, thread by thread. And nobody would know that it wasn't *really* an accident.

I choked back tears. I felt sick to my stomach.

It would be easy to just let go ...

The pole grew closer. The nose of my car was aimed straight for it.

At the very last second, I swerved and let the telephone pole pass me by. I shuttered and shook my head, trying to clear my thoughts. I glanced at the mountain range in the distance, so majestic and beautiful on this early summer day. I knew I didn't have the guts to go through with it; there were too many unknowns. In the end, I didn't *really* want to hurt my family. I just wanted the ache in my heart to go away.

I just wish something could go right for once.

After a few more minutes, the lovely rolling hills flattened out and gave way to the buildings and houses of the next little town on my route. The speed limit slowed, and I stepped on the brakes. As I pulled into the parking lot of the optometrist's office for my next delivery, I practiced my cheerful smile so I'd be ready for the regular office banter.

"Travis, we're always so excited to see you. You always make our day," the office manager would say with an ear-to-ear smile. I'd laugh in reply and ask about her family's planned vacation next week. The doctor would step out and shake my hand and offer me a cold bottle of water to take along, and I would accept. Everything was nice and happy that way. I was well-liked, and I did my job well.

But they didn't know that just 10 minutes earlier, just like every day on this route for the last month, I was a split-second away from killing myself.

❧❧❧

Some things you just don't ever forget.

The living room was dark, and there were a few boxes here and there, as my mom had been preparing to take the four of us kids and move into Grandma's house down in Southern California. Mom and all of us were sleeping in the living room that night; she was lying on the couch, and my sister and two brothers were scattered around the floor. I was under the coffee table, half-asleep, listening to my siblings' heavy breathing.

My dad came in then, reeking of alcohol and in an ugly mood. He and my mom went back and forth, exchanging nasty words about the divorce and about her moving out and how he never cared to see her ever again. Dad could be really mean when he was drunk.

"What about these kids?" Mom pleaded.

The air was still for a long moment.

"I don't give a d*** about these kids."

Under the coffee table, the harsh words hit me like a truck and embedded themselves in my memory forever. I replayed the words over and over again in my mind, and each time, I became a little more crushed. *Daddy doesn't love me anymore.*

It shouldn't have surprised me, I suppose. What had I ever done to deserve his love, anyway? But at the young age of 5, I didn't know any better.

After he left, I lay there in the dark, crying silently. And I'm pretty certain that above me, on the couch, my mom was crying, too.

అఅఅ

We moved in with my grandma, and over the next few years, with the absence of a father-figure, we became very bad kids. We stole from stores, used bad language and got in trouble at school all the time. My mom hardly knew what to do with us.

I still missed my dad terribly, and one day, when I was about 8, I asked Mom if I could call him. I thought that if I could only talk to him, maybe he would remember how much he loved us.

Or maybe I would feel better, just hearing his voice — a voice I could hardly remember anymore.

Mom wrote down his phone number for me on a small piece of notepad paper. I dialed the digits and stood in the kitchen, holding the phone to my ear, waiting for Dad to answer.

"Hello?" The voice on the other end of the line was gruff.

I paused, my nerves starting to get the best of me. I cleared my throat and held the phone tighter.

"Hey, Dad. It's Travis."

Silence.

"Dad?"

"How did you get this number?"

"Mom gave it to me."

"Let me speak with her."

I handed the phone to my mom then. That was the last time I would ever speak to my father as a child.

❧❧❧

On Sundays, my mom began sending us to a local church to attend services. I guess she figured that a little bit of religion might improve our bad behavior. It certainly couldn't hurt.

I was starved for fatherly attention, so I was immediately drawn to the church's youth pastor, John — a black man with a friendly face and squinty eyes that sparkled when he laughed. *Everyone* was important to John. He sat and hung out with the kids for what seemed like hours. There was always a lot of laughter and fun conversation, and I wanted to be right in the middle of it. I wanted to feel loved and accepted by John, too. I wanted to have a good time like the others.

John embraced our family right away. His heart was so big, and he took a real interest in my siblings and me. He told me about God, and within a few months, I decided I wanted to become a Christian like him. I had never looked up to any man the way I looked up to him.

My mom started attending the church, and soon she

and John began dating. Though their relationship never progressed to the point of marriage, John became a permanent fixture in our family, filling the role of father-figure for me for the next 30 years. He was someone I could trust implicitly.

Life was tough on a single mom, and money was hard to come by, so when I was 12, my mom decided to move the family back up to Central California, where she thought the cost of living would be cheaper. John moved, too, getting his own place nearby. Mom got a job as a maid in a motel, but money was still tight. She did the best she could with what she had. There was a period of time during my high school years that we didn't have a church, so John would come over to lead a prayer time for us in our living room on Sunday mornings.

As I got older, I developed an interest in agriculture. Our town was quite rural, so there were plenty of opportunities to learn. In college, I became a competitive "meat judger," winning three national competitions where I was asked to grade cuts of beef, steak, pork and lamb, much like the USDA would. I graduated in 1993 with an Associate's Degree in Agriculture. Because of my meat-judging championships, I was offered several scholarships and job opportunities. My future in the agriculture industry seemed promising.

About that time, John decided he wanted to start a church in our town. It didn't make any sense to my practical mind, but I really felt like I wanted to help John start the church, instead of agricultural pursuits. Because I knew how much the church meant to me after my dad rejected me, I was confident that together we could be a blessing in many people's lives.

So, with some money John received from an auto insurance settlement, we rented a house with a patio and garage that had been converted to business space. We bought a piano, a guitar and some drums. Every Sunday we met there and had church. For the first three months, it was just John, my younger brother, Chris, and me. We would have music sessions, followed by John's teaching from the Bible. It got discouraging that nobody ever came.

"Maybe you're not meant to play," John would say to Chris sometimes, as he beat on his drums.

"Well, maybe you're not meant to teach," Chris teased back.

But people did come eventually. Word spread, and within a short amount of time, we were averaging about 80 people per Sunday. We actually had a church! I was particularly proud of the work we did in the community. Each year, for five years straight, we picked the worst part of the city and set up in a park for a four-hour period, partnering with the police and other community departments. There were game booths and face-painting for kids, and everyone received a toy. We raffled bicycles and food baskets, and we gave everybody a free hotdog and soda. We shared about the love of Jesus Christ. It was a great ministry, and we felt like we were making a difference in people's lives. It was exactly the kind of thing I loved.

The church needed a bigger space to meet, and in the spring of 1999, as we reached a membership of 120 members, we moved into a new, larger building. Things were really going well, and the decision to choose the church over an agriculture career was proving to be a good one. God was blessing me and using me, and wow, did I think I had a lot of talents to be used. The church was on a roll, and for me, the sky was the limit. Or so it seemed.

అఇఇ

By now, I was almost 30, and I felt like I was ready for the next step in my life. I was itching to settle down, get married and start a family. I had met a young woman in the church named Susan, and though John cautioned us that our relationship was moving too quickly, Susan and I became engaged.

I'm a grown man. I'm old enough to make my own decisions.

It did seem fast. But I also felt like my work with the growing church had given me confidence in my ability to know when something was right or wrong. I was certain that *this* was right.

A few weeks before the wedding, I decided to legally change my last name to John's last name. The gesture was an acknowledgement of John's special place in my life. He really had become more than just my youth pastor or my mom's boyfriend or my mentor. Regardless of the difference in our skin color, over the years, John had truly become my dad. Since he had no blood-related children of his own, I felt that taking his last name was a way of honoring the father he had been to my siblings and me.

Susan and I had a big wedding in November of 1999, and because we didn't have enough money for our own place, I had her move into the house I shared with John and my brother Chris. Around this time, John had a heart attack and was diagnosed with diabetes. I felt like it was good that we all lived in the same house together, so I could keep an eye on him.

❧❧❧

Early the next spring, John, Chris and I were doing some yard work one day when Chris started feeling lightheaded.

"I haven't eaten all day. I really don't feel good," he admitted, wiping the sweat off his forehead and taking a seat in the living room, just inside the front door.

"Stay right here, son," John said. "We'll go get something to eat."

John grabbed his keys, and he and I headed for the car.

"Wait! I'll go with you!" Chris shouted out after us, but as he stood to his feet, he blacked out.

Crack.

The sound of my brother's head hitting the doorway was like that of plastic bowls being clapped together.

"Chris!" John and I ran to my brother's side. His eyes

had rolled back into his head, and his body started convulsing.

"He's having a seizure! Travis, call 911!" John shouted.

I ran to the phone and called the ambulance. It all seemed to be happening so quickly. The ambulance arrived and whisked Chris away to the hospital, while John and I followed in his car. Secretly, I was worried about the stress the situation was having on John's health, too.

At the hospital we learned that Chris had regained consciousness but was having trouble with his memory. Though he was treated and released, Chris experienced seizures, frequent falling and memory loss for the next couple of months. The living situation became stressful for all of us. John developed high blood pressure and then started having trouble with back pain, for which he took muscle relaxants. Together, they were a mess.

Through all of this, we were still trying to manage our church. Since Chris could not perform his church duties, more weight fell on me. I spent more and more time at church and less time at home with Susan. Some days I thought I might as well live there.

John started taking muscle relaxers in order to sleep at night and to function during the day. His need for the pills was becoming an addiction. The church members started noticing a change in his personality. John was quick to tell people he was on heavy medication. Sometimes I felt like he was too open with everyone about his faults.

People began losing respect for John and leaving the

church. They said horrible things about us, and it was extremely hurtful. We had poured our lives into these people, and for what? This? A tarnished image? Hatred? As the church lost members, it also lost money, and it became harder and harder for us to make the monthly rent payment on our building. Everything was spinning out of control.

Susan withdrew from both the church and from me. I tried to discuss it with her, but a wall had grown between us. I realized I had my priorities all wrong. I had been putting my work at the church before my relationship with my wife, which had been extremely hurtful to her. As a new bride, she hadn't been happy living with my family, and I hadn't even noticed.

Unfortunately, my sudden interest in our marriage was too little, too late. I was adamant that divorce was not an option for us, so in a last-ditch effort, I got a second job as a courier so we would have the money to get an apartment and move out of the house we'd been sharing with John and Chris. At Susan's request, I also tried to commit myself to fewer church activities.

Why are we having all these battles?

I had a lot of time to think while I was driving my courier routes, and I would often mull over all the things that were going wrong.

We're faithful! We're doing everything we're supposed to be doing. I've spent all this time telling people about you, God, but now you're nowhere to be found!

No matter how much I prayed to God to help us, the

battles kept coming. Everything was getting worse. My father-figure was struggling with addiction and illness. My brother was also battling for his health. My marriage was failing fast. And the church we had labored hard to grow was falling apart. I had a sick feeling in the pit of my stomach. I was depressed. I wanted out. And every day on Highway 65, I struggled with thoughts of taking my own life.

God, if you don't help me, then I'm going to go through with this, I'd threaten nearly every single day.

"Stay Alive on Highway 65"?

Whatever.

శ్రీశ్రీశ్రీ

On a warm summer day in July, I was making local deliveries for my courier job, when a simple stop at a stoplight turned into a major collision. My company vehicle was rear-ended, leaving me with a severe case of whiplash.

Of course, I thought bitterly. *What else could go wrong?*

The pain of the whiplash was bad, so I went to see the doctor. He prescribed Vicodin and eight months of physical therapy.

"You will always deal with this pain from the whiplash," he said, scribbling out the prescription on his stationery pad. "It probably won't ever go away."

For the first time, I actually kind of sympathized with

John's back pain. I understood his need for the muscle relaxers.

Sometimes you've gotta do what you gotta do to get through the day.

Because of the accident and the medication I was on, my company decided it was best if I no longer drove my usual daily route on Highway 65. They gave me a desk job and kept me in the office. I was secretly grateful, since I had become fearful of the dangerous road and of what I might decide to do to myself on any given day. It was hard enough to "Stay Alive on Highway 65" when you *wanted* to, much less when you didn't.

I had a lot of unanswered questions. I didn't understand how, when I had chosen an occupation that I felt God wanted, everything was going so wrong. I had done my best, and I had done a good job. But with my family's deteriorating health and subsequent addiction, the financial problems, the failing marriage, the church struggles, the newly added chronic pain on top of it all — I didn't know what to believe anymore.

Maybe we got this whole thing wrong.

ॐॐॐ

The white Cadillac pulled into the driveway of John's tiny house. Chris didn't live there anymore; the church congregation had dwindled to 40, so Chris had lost interest, met a girl and decided to do something else with his life. Now John and I were sitting in the living room, talking on a Saturday afternoon. The door of the Cadillac slammed shut, and I peeked through the blinds to see Gordon, one of our former church board members, walking toward the front door.

I looked back at John, sitting in the recliner. "It's Gordon."

"Oh, no," he groaned. "Why is *he* here?"

It hit me how *tired* John was looking these days. Old, too. The doorbell rang, and I reluctantly made my way to the door to open it.

"Why, hello, Travis," Gordon greeted me, casually. "Is your dad at home?"

"Sure. Come on in."

Gordon was extraordinarily tall and skinny; he had to duck under the doorframe so he wouldn't hit his head. I noticed right away that the look on his face was one of worry and concern. Somehow I didn't think this was meant to be a pleasant social call.

"Hi, Gordon, sit down." John struggled to his feet and extended his hand out for Gordon to shake. But Gordon ignored it and sat on the sofa across the room.

John shot me a panicked look that said, *What are we going to hear now?* I pulled up a chair next to him. I didn't want him to be alone on the end of whatever Gordon had come to say.

Gordon didn't mince any words.

"I feel like the Lord sent me over here to tell you folks that God is not pleased with you. That's why this is all happening to you."

I felt, more than saw, John's body become tense next to mine.

Gordon gestured to the Cadillac parked in the driveway. "See that Caddy my brother-in-law gave me? If you live right, like I do," he continued, "*that's* what God does to you. Blessing, not cursing."

John leaned forward in his chair and locked eyes with him.

"Get out of my house." John's words came out slow and clear. He was working hard to control his temper.

"But, brother ..."

"You're no brother of mine."

I stood then, hoping Gordon would follow my lead. Thankfully, he did. I opened the door for him, and as he ducked his head back under, he paused and looked over his shoulder at John.

"You know I meant no harm. I'm just trying to help."

With that, Gordon sauntered over to his shiny oversized car. I shut the door firmly behind him.

How dare Gordon come in here and say those things? We were already bombarded with those thoughts — wondering what we were doing wrong. We didn't need board members coming in here and flaunting what God was doing for them while our lives seemed to be falling apart, piece by piece.

John buried his face in his hands and began to weep. In all the years I had known him, I had never seen John cry like this. It was the cry of a broken man.

I wished with all my heart that I could cry. But all I felt

was anger and indignation — at Gordon, at God, at everyone.

๛๛๛

My divorce from Susan became final in July of 2002. Even though it had been a year since the accident, the pain from the whiplash was getting worse. I became dependent on Vicodin to get me through each day. Even if I woke up feeling better, I would take the pills in anticipation of the pain.

Still, despite my anger and doubts about God, I continued working at the church. John had taught me to never *blame* God for things; that's dangerous ground to walk on, he said. So though I had a lot of anger and many, many questions, I kept plugging on.

One particular Sunday, I was teaching an adult Sunday school class in our church sanctuary room. I was speaking about the responsibilities within a relationship with God and the importance of being faithful to him. It was a topic I personally struggled with, of course, so I felt like I was preaching to myself, too. When I was done with my sermon, I asked if there were any questions.

At the very back of the room, John sat in one of the ushers' chairs, behind the faded green pews. He lifted his hand.

"John?" I motioned to him.

He was quiet for a second, then squinted his eyes at me. It was a look of disappointment.

"So, you're saying that even when your wife is struggling and asks you to stop being so involved in the church, you should still be faithful? You shouldn't let her stop you from doing what God wants you to do, right?"

His words pierced my heart.

Seriously? You're coming out against me in front of the church? I've been here with you, side by side, and we've worked through all this stuff together. And this is the thanks I get?

I thought these things, but I said nothing. I glanced at the congregation, sitting silently in the pews, waiting almost breathlessly for my response. I felt sick. I felt like the walls of the sanctuary were closing in on me. I had never been so embarrassed in my entire life. Worse still, the only father I'd ever trusted was attacking me.

I thumped my Bible shut and walked down the center aisle toward the double doors. As I reached the back of the sanctuary, Brother Dave, one of our church deacons, stood up from where he was seated next to John.

"Come on, you guys," he pleaded, putting a hand on each of our shoulders. "Not like this."

But I wasn't in a mood to play nice.

"Sorry. I can't do this anymore."

I pushed past him and walked straight out of the building. The sun was bright, and my eyes were filled with tears, so it took me a second to adjust to the daylight. I stumbled in the direction of my car.

Never had I felt so alone. I felt completely and utterly betrayed. Up until that point, I had trusted that John would be there for me, no matter what. We had been in this thing together.

I have absolutely nobody now. This is the second dad I've lost.

I jammed my keys into the ignition and drove as fast as I could to the most isolated place I could think of: a cornfield by the airport. There, I sat weeping and crying for hours.

"I don't want to live anymore, God! It's too much!"

So this is what it feels like to completely hit rock bottom, I thought.

I was at a point of absolute desperation. And that's when it hit me. By looking to John to fill my desperate need for a father, I overlooked the most loyal, loving father of all — *God.* John wasn't the only one who had adopted me. God had adopted me, too.

My biological father was, without a doubt, human, and now I saw that John was, too. Suddenly the Bible verse, Psalm 68:5, became very real to me. It tells us that God is a "father to the fatherless." All these years, I had served the church of John and not the church of God.

Oh, God, please forgive me! Please be my father! Please be my dad!

Peace washed over me. I felt safe. I felt like everything was going to be okay. People would fail me, but God wouldn't. Maybe, just maybe, God had allowed me to hit the lowest point in my life, just so I could see how much I needed *him* even more than I needed John.

ॐॐॐ

In the days that followed, John asked for my forgiveness. It was hard for me. The pain of his words and the embarrassment I had felt were still very raw. But he was so insistent that he was wrong, and even though I knew now that I had been putting more trust in John than in God, I didn't want our relationship to end. So with a lot of caution and reservation, I chose to let it go.

In fact, there seemed to be a big change in John. He went to many church members' houses, Gordon's included, and cried, begging for forgiveness — for letting his addiction problems get the better of him, for not keeping his eyes on Jesus, for not being the leader he should have been.

I didn't understand. "Why are you asking *them* for forgiveness? They're the ones who turned their backs on us."

"Travis, putting your own feelings and emotions on the table is more important than anything else to breaking down those walls and bringing healing," he answered.

I thought about the Jesus I had preached all those years. The people he had served and loved beat him and nailed him to a cross. Even as he died a slow and terrible death at the hands of his betrayers, he cried out, "Father, forgive them, for they do not know what they are doing" (Luke 23:34). I felt justified in my anger. But I knew I must forgive those who betrayed me, too.

Even as a pastor, I had decided a couple of years before

that I didn't like people anymore. People can be cruel and hateful at times. They can make horrible mistakes based on ugly emotions. But now I realized that people are only human. All of us, including myself, fall short of perfection. Like Jesus said, we don't realize what we are doing. I thought I was drawn to *John's* love for me. Now I realized it was *Jesus'* love reaching out to me through John.

Had John and I both made mistakes? Of course we had. But now, John was asking forgiveness from Jesus and from others. He was letting God change his heart. He was offering Jesus' love and forgiveness to the people who had hurt him.

Maybe Jesus can do that in me, too.

ৰ্চ ৰ্চ ৰ্চ

"Look, if you can't manage the rent on this facility, you may need to admit to yourselves that the smaller building is a wiser choice."

A pastor friend of John's had come to speak at our church. He prayed with us and recommended that we move back into the smaller church building/house we had been in originally. It was a hard decision. It felt like admitting defeat. But as we had learned the hard way, this was God's church — not ours.

After we moved in 2003, we knew it was time to refocus the church's vision again. We started the community outreaches back up. It was good to be reaching out to people again, but I felt like an idiot. In the early days, my attitude had been, "Look at all I'm doing for God!" Now it was: "I screwed up my life and doubted God; what makes me think I can help people?"

Though I felt like a failure, I knew one thing: *I loved Jesus so much.* My pride had been crushed, but I had never felt closer to God in my life than I did right then. He was so merciful to me, and I had an inner peace I had never known. I understood that God had never been interested in *crushing* me; he just wanted to sweep out what needed to be fixed.

"The old clay isn't thrown away," I heard T.D. Jakes, another minister, say on television. "God uses the same clay; he just remolds and reshapes it."

That was exactly how I felt.

❧❧❧

Surprisingly, things settled down. The church was finally doing well and accomplishing its original God-given purpose. It wasn't growing, but it was stable. It had been a couple of years since my divorce, and I was praying about the possibility of God providing me with a wife and family.

On a Saturday in August of 2004, I helped set up the church's meeting area for a baby shower. I arranged tables and chairs for the ladies and watched as they hung streamers and prepared appetizers and punch for the guests. I was the only male in the building, in the midst of a dozen happy women, buzzing with their chatter.

Suddenly, a beautiful brunette caught my eye. She was giving the mother-to-be a hug and handing her a nicely wrapped gift with ribbons and bows. She was absolutely gorgeous.

Lord, that woman right there? That's her! That's the one I want to marry!

She was so pleasant and happy; I couldn't keep my eyes off of her.

"Pastor Travis?" The grandmother-to-be tapped me on the shoulder. "You don't have to stay. We've got everything set up and ready to go. Thanks so much for your help!"

"Oh, no," I answered. "I don't have anything else going on this afternoon. I'd be happy to stay around and help out as needed."

The lady shrugged and went back to the shower while I puttered around between the kitchen and meeting room, wiping tables and finding tasks to keep me busy. My eyes never left the pretty girl with the dark hair as she played the party games, praised the adorable baby gifts and laughed with friends over a piece of cake.

"I'm Travis," I finally had the guts to say, right as she was collecting her purse and keys. "I haven't seen you around here before and wanted to introduce myself."

"I'm Melissa." She smiled brightly.

"Do you have a church? We'd love for you to attend here." I hoped I didn't sound too enthusiastic.

"Well, maybe I'll try it out. It was nice to meet you …"

"Travis," I said, filling in the blank. "Travis."

❧❧❧

A week later, Melissa walked into the church on Sunday morning, holding two adorable dark-haired little girls by the hand. She was even more stunning than I had remembered.

"Good morning," she said, smiling, and my heart nearly leapt out of my chest.

Through the grapevine, I learned that Melissa had gone through a terrible divorce. I asked her out, and as we dated, she shared with me how she had been raised Catholic, how she had gone through a lot in her life and how her faith in God had helped her get through an alcohol addiction. Now she had a good job and a house, and she was, I thought, a strong, amazing single mother. I was falling in love.

"I feel good in my spirit about this one," John said a few months later, when I told him I was thinking of proposing to Melissa. "I think she's the one."

Melissa and I married in September of 2005. My heart was filled with thankfulness to God for giving me such a lovely wife and two beautiful daughters. I felt completely undeserving. But the blessing wasn't over yet; the following August, Melissa gave birth to our baby girl. In two years' time, I had gone from being alone in my apartment to living in a house, in love, surrounded by four amazing women.

Life was indescribably good.

No Easy Road

I pulled our car into the driveway of the Baileys' house. The Baileys were our friends; Melissa had met Karen at work, and Karen's husband, Rod, was a deputy sheriff. We enjoyed frequent get-togethers at each other's homes. Colorful Christmas lights hung from the eave over the garage, and my heart felt sick inside. Melissa and I exchanged a look: *He hung those lights, and now he's gone.* I reached for her hand as a tear trickled down her cheek.

"God, please help us to be a blessing to this family," I prayed. "Let us bring *your* peace into this home, in the midst of the grief."

Since we had gotten the phone call a couple hours ago, it hadn't really sunk in that Rod was gone … our friend, shot and killed in the line of duty. It was sudden and unexpected, as those things always are, but now, as we were ready to face Karen and the family, it was becoming real.

We stayed with them briefly to pray with them, hug them and offer our help. Throughout the week, we spent a lot of time with the family, encouraging and helping them.

"What about the service?" someone asked. "Could you perform the funeral service?"

It was the least I could do. That week, I had multiple meetings with the sheriff's office, helping to plan the funeral for my friend.

I prayed, as I always did, that my presence would bring

the peace of Jesus — less of me and more of him.

"Have you ever considered being a chaplain for the sheriff's office?" a lieutenant asked me the evening before the funeral.

"No, I haven't," I answered.

"I think you'd be a good fit. You should think about it."

That wasn't the last time I heard that. After the funeral, a pastor at a larger church also came to me and suggested I become a chaplain.

Maybe I should look into this.

After some prayer about it, Melissa and I felt like I should apply for a chaplain job and see what happened. I applied for one with the police department and one with the sheriff's office, and in 2008, I got the job with the sheriff's office. I was thrilled.

Over the next couple of years, I loved my chaplain job. I enjoyed going out and accompanying the deputies on calls, sharing the love of Jesus and having tons of opportunities to pray for people. To my surprise, however, I found myself actually falling in love with the deputy job itself. I was seriously considering going to the police academy.

There was just one problem. I was still taking Vicodin regularly. I had a severe addiction. I was taking so much Vicodin (and had been for so many years) that I didn't know how much pain I was really in anymore. How much of it was pain, and how much of it was fear I was going to be in pain? That was the question.

God, I'm worried. With the guns we handle, people in law enforcement cannot be on drugs.

God had done so much for me, yet this was the one big thing I had been holding on to. I hadn't wanted him to take this from me, just in case it meant pain for the rest of my life. But now I knew that in order to move on and grasp hold of everything he had for me, my prescription pain medication had to go. I needed to be free.

I made an appointment with my doctor.

"You're going to have withdrawal symptoms," the doctor warned. "It's going to be very difficult. But I think you're making the right choice."

God, please help me.

The doctor lowered my dose, and over a three-month period, I was progressively weaned off *all* my pain medication. The real miracle was that I didn't experience withdrawal after all. God had cleansed my system, and the pain was more manageable than I had imagined it would be. When I entered the police academy in February of 2010, I was completely drug free.

❧❧❧

At the age of 38, I was the oldest person to graduate from the police academy. With God's help, I also graduated first in my class. Two weeks later, I landed a job as a paid deputy sheriff.

It amazed me how much easier things were when I let God direct my life, rather than trying to control everything myself. I wanted to be a man following after God's heart, just like King David in the Bible (1 Samuel 13:14). As great of a godly man as David was, he was still extremely human and made some pretty horrible decisions. But because his heart was right, God still used him.

I often thought of myself like that. I was still that same lump of clay that had become too prideful about the church I'd helped build … that made bad decisions in my first marriage … that let an addiction take over my life … that began to hate people and doubt God. *That same lump of clay.* But I had been cleaned out, remolded, reshaped and repurposed.

Thank God for his mercy.

❧❧❧

"Hey, Dad," I greeted John, planting a kiss on his weathered cheek. The hair at his temples was white, and there were more specks of white all over his head than I remembered. He was aging.

"Travis." His eyes lit up, and he adjusted his wheelchair so he could face me where I had sat down on the couch. He reached a hand down to rub the stump of his leg, which had been amputated a few years back.

We no longer attended John's church. It had been a hard choice to make, but Melissa and I had felt like we were ready for the next step. Our new church, Bethel Family Worship Center, had an amazing kids' ministry that our girls really enjoyed. We were learning and growing as well. There weren't any hard feelings; John had understood.

"I stopped by to change that kitchen light bulb for you," I told him, holding up the bulb in my hand.

John nodded gratefully. "Thank you."

I took a look around the familiar living room; it needed a good cleaning. There were old newspapers and empty drinking glasses cluttering the coffee table. The lamp was on, even though there was plenty of daylight streaming in through the front window. And, as always, John's Bible lay open on the dusty TV tray. His Bible was always, always handy.

"Travis." John squinted at me. "Jesus said he's coming for me soon."

"No, don't say that! You've got kids and grandkids to live for."

John shook his head slowly, but not necessarily out of sadness. "No, I mean it. He told me he's coming for me soon."

I swallowed hard. Who was I to contradict what Jesus told John?

"Well, then, I guess you'll be ready to go," I said, attempting a smile.

I stood then and headed to the kitchen to change the light bulb. Before I left, I spent a few more minutes talking to John, reminiscing about old times and sharing the latest antics of his three granddaughters. He listened to my stories and laughed.

"Tell them I love them," he said, a twinkle in his eye.

"I will," I promised.

৵৵৵

Two weeks later, we stopped at the coast on the way home from a family vacation to Disneyland. Sitting on the beach, I got the call. John had passed away.

I clapped my cell phone shut and sat cross-legged on the sand.

"I can't believe he's gone." My eyes took in the beauty of the Pacific Ocean, the waves crashing against the beach. My daughters were busy making a sand castle several yards in front of us.

"I know. I'm so sorry." Melissa's voice caught on her tears. "How did he go?"

"Heart attack. They said it was sudden, and there was no pain."

"Good," she whispered, taking my hand.

God, thank you for John's presence in my life.

That afternoon, we packed up our car and prepared to head home. There was a celebration of John's life to plan, after all.

Our car smelled of ocean water, sweat and sunscreen; a film of sand covered the floorboard. All were signs of a good trip.

The road home was across the valley from Highway 65, but the gorgeous scenery was the same. The wildflowers of late summer covered the green hills, and deer frolicked in the distance. The mountains were an amazing backdrop against the clear blue sky.

Oh, God, this feels so good — driving this road with my beautiful family and wanting to live.

"So, girls, how about we stop for a treat?"

My suggestion was met with a chorus of girlish cheers from the entire brood in the backseat.

I reached my hand to my face and wiped away tears of gratitude for God's amazing mercy and love.

SECOND CHANCES
The Story of Candis
Written by Miranda Koerner

"Let me out!" I pounded my fists against the dark wooden door, my frenzied panting echoing in the dark closet. "Come on, let me out!"

"Why should we?" Giggling leaked in under the door, drowning out my captor's muffled taunts. "You're the one who likes the closet!"

"Let us out!" My fists slammed against the door, my forearms aching. "If you don't let us out, I'll scream."

"I don't like it in here." My little sister, Sarah, tugged on my sleeve, her dark eyes wide. "Get us out, Candis."

"Maybe you should let them out." My sister Mary's quiet voice snuck in under the door, a whisper of reason between the neighbor boys' snickers.

"Fine. Mom will be home soon, anyway." The door jerked open, bright light blasting me. Narrowing my eyes, I glared at the smirking neighborhood boy. "Oh, quit being such a baby. It was funny."

He nudged my sister. "Isn't it, Mary?" I stared at her, but she said nothing, staring at the floor. He laughed. "At least one of you is fun. Stupid girls. Remember, if you tell your mom about this …" He shook his fist, and I shrank back. "Let's just say, your sisters really won't like coming over here, then."

"You wouldn't dare hurt them."

"Don't tempt me." Shoving me back into the closet, his laughter followed him down the hall, searching out his next easy mark. Shivering, I blinked back tears as his older sister, Nancy, escorted us to the bathroom to wipe them away.

"Why do they think this is so funny?" My voice was flat as I helped Sarah out of the closet, her small arms trembling as she reached for my help.

"You know how boys play, Candis." Nancy dabbed Sarah's cheeks with a soft rag, then reached for me. I jerked back, refusing to let the comforting rag wash away my tears. "Don't worry, my mom's on her way home. There's no need to bother her or your mom with this, is there?"

My two sisters shook their heads. Sighing, I bent mine. "I guess not," I muttered.

"Good. Let's go to the kitchen, and I will get you a snack before the boys eat it all." Nancy took my sisters' hands, and off they went. Trailing behind them, my heart twisted with every step.

But no matter how the words simmered inside, my lips would never spill them.

❧❧❧❧

No one treated me too differently than my sisters, even though I was a head taller with fair skin.

I was doomed to bathe in sunscreen or suffer a painful

sunburn, unlike my sisters who had perfect California tans.

After years of infertility, my parents chose to adopt me. When I was less than a year old, the seemingly impossible happened; my mother conceived, and I became a big sister to Mary. My sister Sarah was born into our family two years later.

Gratefully, my parents were very open about my adoption. Kids knew I was adopted, but it was no big deal. Between swimming in my neighbor's pool, going to barbecues and crashing adult poker games, I was just one of the kids on our cul-de-sac.

As far as the world was concerned, we were the perfect family. When others would ask my mother if it was different with Mary or Sarah, she would just smile. "We have three daughters," she replied. "We love each of them exactly the same." Years later, I would know just what she meant.

By the time I was 5, my parents divorced. Luckily, it wasn't one of those big dramatic divorces where each parent was fighting for every last right they could hold on to. Our parents always seemed to put the needs of my sisters and me above their issues.

Aside from the jerk neighborhood boys, who thankfully moved out of town, I could not have asked for a better childhood. My mom worked long hours as a legal secretary and took on odd typing jobs at home while caring for my sisters and me at the same time. My mother let the local Baptist church bus take my sisters and I to church and vacation Bible school. She stayed home, to catch some well-deserved time for herself.

My childhood was carefree until my father remarried for the second time.

At first, I liked my new stepfamily. I really did. A compliant, quiet kid, I always tried to do the right thing, be helpful and never wanted anything to be my fault.

It made me the perfect target. And my new stepsister, Marie, took full advantage.

"This is how it's going to be," she hissed one night. She had stepped out of the shower and grabbed me before I could reach for my toothbrush. Her forceful fingers dug into my arm, nearly piercing the bone. Her dark eyes bored into me, wild and full of dark rage. "You're never going to tell anyone what I tell you to do, okay?"

All I could do was stutter, "But …"

"You can't tell anyone." Her lips curled up, twisting in a leer. "You don't want me to be mad, do you?"

I shook my head, swallowing my fear.

"Good." Grabbing my head, she thrust it between her bare breasts. The towel dropped between us, draping over my feet. My sisters' happy chatter rang out down the hall, their laughter sounding far away and foreign. My heart pounded in my ears, my stomach twisting. My mind raced, spiraling with the same thoughts: *This is wrong. This is bad. This needs to stop.*

But my lips sealed shut, my fears shut inside. I just did whatever she forced me to do. Things no child should ever have to do.

As Marie grew more and more demanding, jerking me in her room while my sisters were playing, I tried to find ways to get out of going to my dad's when it was his visitation weekend.

"I don't want to go," I whined to my mom, my little overnight bag stubbornly empty. "I don't like it there."

"You have to go." My mom barely glanced up, scanning over her next typing job. "Your dad misses you."

"No, he doesn't. He just has Marie watch us so he can go to the office to work."

My mother raised an eyebrow, eyeing me.

"Candis, what's the real problem?"

I bit my lip. I wanted to tell. I knew I should tell. But my lips wouldn't move. The words wouldn't come; they were shoved so deep, my tongue lay still. Finally, I blurted out the only thing that came to mind. "I don't like Marie. She's mean." *And makes me do things I don't want to do,* I added silently.

"I know, honey. I know it's hard. But sometimes we have to do things we don't want to do."

She didn't need to tell me twice. "But, Mom …"

"No buts, honey. It would break your dad's heart if you didn't go. Okay?" Mom ruffled my fair hair, kissing my forehead. As far as she was concerned, the matter was settled.

"Okay," I sighed, gnawing on my lip. As far as I was concerned, Saturday could stay as many days away as possible. When the dreaded day came, I glued myself to my dad's side, avoiding the smoldering glare from Marie's dark eyes. At bath time I hurried through my bath, brushing my teeth and scrubbing my face at the same time. Jerking a comb through my hair, I was struggling into my pajamas when nails dug into my shoulder. I froze, my pajamas clinging to my still-wet body.

"Going somewhere?" Marie growled.

"I …"

"Shut up." She jerked me closer, dropping the towel. "You haven't told anyone, have you?"

I shook my head, wincing as she grabbed it between her hands. I closed my eyes, gritting my teeth. Soon it would be over. Soon it would be over, and I could go to bed. "Girls?" My eyes flew open. My father was staring at Marie, his face twisted in concern. "Marie, what's going on?"

Marie flushed, bending down and grabbing her towel. "We were just playing."

My father glanced at me. His jaw tightened. "I don't think so." Handing me a clean towel, he lowered his voice. "Candis, why don't you go to bed? Marie and I are going to have a little talk."

"I didn't tell," I whispered, clutching the towel as I raced down the hall. Tearing the covers off my bed, I leaped inside. I clutched my pillow over my face, shielding myself from the murmur of voices in the hall.

"I was quiet," I whispered in the dark, my tears soaking into the soft pillowcase. "I was nice. I never said anything."

Marie never touched me after that night. She and Dad

acted as if nothing happened, never mentioning the bathroom that night. It would be years before I would ever discuss it with anyone, years before anyone knew the pain Marie had caused me. And it would be decades before I would know that the guilt and shame were never my burden to bear.

She never even said she was sorry.

ॐॐॐ

After graduating high school, where I was active in youth group and church, I ventured out into the real world, getting a job and having as much fun as possible with my friends. Scared and uncertain, I left behind the principles I'd learned at church and did what all my friends were doing, going out and meeting people. At a mutual friend's party one day, I met the man who would change my life.

The only thing I liked more than Dan's green eyes was his smile. He made me laugh, and I was hopelessly devoted in an instant, spending almost every moment with him. He was the only boy I'd been truly crazy about. I was barely in my 20s, but I knew he was the one for me. Before I knew it, we were exchanging vows at the Catholic church Dan's family attended. At the reception, my dad gave the most adoring toast a father could give to a daughter; there wasn't a dry eye in the house. He slid up to me and kissed my cheek. "Congratulations, Candis."

I grinned, giddy to be a new wife.

"I can't believe we're married!"

"I know you'll be happy." My dad patted my shoulder, smiling. "I always wanted you to marry a strong family man with a good job. He'll be good for you."

Tears pricked my eyes, and I smiled through my tears. "He'll be a good dad."

"I know he will." My dad stretched out his hand, coaxing me onto the dance floor. "Let's celebrate. To health, happiness and family!"

Just like my dad hoped, family came sooner than later. In 1992, our daughter, Karen, was born. Less than two years later, our son, Randy, was born. With two babies, two jobs and a bustling house with two cars, we were the picture of perfection. But underneath the image of the perfect American family, everything was falling apart. Dan and I were more friends and parents than husband and wife. We joked and laughed together, but I didn't fall asleep with my head on his shoulder or crave the comfort of his arms after a long day. I was so busy working and raising our babies that I barely noticed as Dan slipped into another life where drinking and drugs were the norm.

At first, he would call and say he needed to stay late after working at his job an hour away. Then he would call and ask if he could go out with the guys — just a drink or two. A drink or two turned into two or three in the morning, then a whole night and eventually an entire week. Soon he stayed at a friend's apartment in Bakersfield during the week, coming home on weekends. It wasn't until I found out I was pregnant with our third child,

David, that I found out about the other woman.

One night, Dan came home and passed out, like he usually did. With the whole house sleeping, I grabbed his truck keys and drove to my sister's house. In her driveway under the honest glare of floodlights, I ripped his truck apart. Everything I knew but never wanted to admit spilled at my feet, evidence I couldn't deny. Seething, I drove home and marched into the house. Dan was standing at the counter, bleary eyed. He blinked at me as I slammed into the kitchen.

"Who is she?"

"Who is who?" His voice was hoarse with sleep and confusion.

"Dan, I know." I exhaled. "I know everything."

"There's nothing going on." He turned away. "There's nothing to know."

"Oh, really?" Grabbing the bag I had carried inside, I shook it out over the counter. Drugs and papers scattered, tumbling over the edge and onto the floor. "I cleaned out your truck. I saw the letters, the drugs. What else are you into — crack, marijuana? Who is she? Are you sleeping with her?"

"She's just a friend." Dan sneered at the mess on the counter. "She's just someone I go out with. She's fun."

"Because I'm so boring?" I raised my voice. "I'm so sorry that I have to work and clean and take care of the kids and not go out drinking all night with you. I have other priorities right now." I gestured toward my bulging stomach.

Dan shifted, not meeting my eyes. "I think I should stay at my friend's place in Bakersfield for a while."

"You do that." Turning away, I blinked back tears. "Stay there with your girlfriend and friends."

"I don't need this." Dan grabbed his wallet and keys. "I'm gone."

Before I could respond, he walked out of the door and out of our lives.

As his taillights faded into the night, my tears fell. Pulling the curtain shut, I collapsed into bed and sobbed. Behind the curtain, my heart was breaking, and my family was shattered.

With Dan gone, the days became a huge blur. I got up, hauled the kids to school, went to work, came home and made dinner and tended to the kids until it was time to go to bed. Everything was the same, but everything was different. As my belly grew, so did my stress. My stomach growled, but I couldn't take a single bite at dinner. It felt as though the baby had wrapped my intestines around his fists and was squeezing, holding on as hard as I was holding on to Dan. Even after David was born in 1997, everything stayed the same. Except now, I had an infant to raise without a father.

In tears, I called my dad. "I can't do this," I told him. "I'm going to get a divorce. I can't believe I'm going to be a single mom. I never thought I'd be like Mom — a single mom with three kids."

My dad sighed into the phone. "Candis, you don't want to do that."

I sniffled. "This is all my fault. I should have never — if I'd been better, if I'd gone out with him …"

"He still would have gotten the drugs. You didn't do anything. Why do you think this is your fault?" my dad asked. "Why do you feel like you're not loveable? You deserve so much more."

My head was reeling with crazy thoughts: *I just … my birth dad didn't want me, why would my husband want me? You left Mom, and now he left me.* I knew the words would hurt my dad, so I kept them to myself.

"You are very special to your mom and me, Candis." My dad's voice wrapped around me like a warm blanket. "You were what we hoped and prayed for. And we hoped you'd find a good husband, a man to treat you well." His words cracked. "Don't give up too soon, Candis. Don't give up too soon, like I did."

Neither of my parents ever expressed regret for their divorce. His words caught my attention. "I will hang on as long as I can and pray Dan makes some changes for the better. I don't think I can do this alone."

But I wouldn't have to. A few weeks later, the kids played outside with the neighborhood kids. Smiling, I shaded my eyes and called, "Who wants a juice box?"

"We do!" They beamed, sprinting through the green grass. "Please, Mom?"

"I'll go get it," I called. Humming to myself, I pulled open the screen door and froze. A pond was forming in my house as water ran out from the bathroom. Wading across the carpet, I burst into tears. Water spewed from the toilet, soaking the carpet and rising up the furniture legs. The hallway was soaked, a sponge of carpet. Squishing my way across the carpet, tears streamed down my face as I inspected the damage. Half of the house was flooded; this would take hours to dry out. For the rest of the day, I moved furniture and set up giant fans to dry the carpet and floors. The clock struck midnight. I hit my knees, exhaustion washing over me.

"Please, God," I begged. "Please help me. I can't do this alone anymore." Tears streamed down my face. "Please," I begged. "Please help me. Please give me the strength to do this."

Sobbing, I lifted my face. Peace soaked into my soul, a soft warm glow glittering over my skin. For the first time in months, I slept like a baby. For the first time in months, I didn't feel alone.

And for the first time in my life, I felt loved. Really loved.

☙ ☙ ☙ ☙

"Are you sure you want to do this?" Dan stood outside my car window, shielding his eyes from the sun.

I shrugged. "You haven't been home in months, Dan. What does it matter if we're divorced or not?" I bit the inside of my cheek. "Especially because you're with her." My heart twisted. The first mistress had been hard. The second one was worse.

"But I just …" He sighed, his shoulders drooping.

"I don't want my kids to think I'm leaving them."

"My parents were divorced," I reminded him. "I turned out fine." A million thoughts ran through my mind, a million things I wanted to say lingering on my lips. *We're more friends than spouses. You don't look at me with love in your eyes. We're parents and buddies. You don't come to my arms; you go to hers. You don't come to me; you go to your drugs.*

I reached down and handed him the papers. "Here are the divorce papers, and I am ready to file them; I just need to know if you even want any type of custody of the kids."

He stared at the papers in my hand. A tear coursed down his stubbled cheek, and his breath caught in his throat. "I can't do it."

"You don't want to see them at all?" I gripped the steering wheel. "Not even on weekends?"

"I can't get divorced." His fingers wrapped around mine. The papers fluttered across my lap, falling in the baseboards of the car. "I want to be a family. I want to come back home."

My heart pounded, my fingers tingling. "But things can't be the same," I told him. "We need help. You need help. You need support, not drugs. Not *her.*"

"I'll get help." Dan kissed my fingers, the eyes I'd always loved shining. "I'll get help."

Just as fast as we had started and lost a family, we came together again. Dan went to Bethel Family Worship Center to watch a dramatic performance that brought about a dramatic change in him. He asked God to forgive his failures and past. And then he determined to make things right with me and our children.

As hard as he had thrown himself into drugs, he threw himself into becoming the good husband and father my dad had always wanted for me. Dan even volunteered, taught Sunday school and met with a group of other Christian men once a week.

Slowly, our family became what I always wanted. We went to church, were active on weekends and laughed again. Dan and I were closer, but not as close as I would have liked. But with our focus on the kids, I ignored the empty space in our marriage. *This is just what happens when you have kids,* I told myself. *Things will get better later.* The last thing I wanted to do was to rock the boat, to have Dan leave again. The kids were happy, Dan was happy and I was happier than I had been in a long time. I had hope; that was all that mattered. I'd gotten a second chance at a family, and I wouldn't do anything to disrupt that again.

But six years after we'd restored our family, we'd be ripped apart in a way none of us could imagine.

ᷛᷛᷛᷛ

"Mom, Mom, guess what!" David ran inside, beaming. My sweet green-eyed angel, he looked like a miniature Dan but with blond hair. David was my child, my buddy. We were the two that didn't like sports, that loved singing and dancing.

Wrapping my arms around him, I kissed his head. "What, sweet baby boy?"

He beat his bare chest and crowed, "We're barbecuing! We're the HNC!"

"What's that, baby?" I laughed. David's laugh stole my heart every time.

"The half-naked chefs!" He danced around, grinning as I giggled. "We're going to go swimming after we grill!"

"Is Daddy going to take you?"

"Yup!" He beat his skinny pale chest. "Are you coming?"

"I can't, baby. I have to take food to a lady from church." I kissed his cheek and rumpled his hair. "I'll see you in a little bit."

If only I'd known I wouldn't.

Thirty minutes later, checking out at the grocery store, I sighed and fished out my ringing phone. "Hello?"

"Candis?" Dan's voice cracked over the line.

I froze. "What happened?"

"You've got to get here. There's been an accident."

Grabbing my change, I sprinted out the door. "Where are you? Where are you?"

"At the stoplight at the corner by the house. The kids and I were going swimming. My light was green, and this car was going full speed right at us, he didn't see the red light, he was on his phone, and his car hit us …" His voice shuddered. "Hurry."

I jerked open my car door, twisting the key as the engine roared to life. "I'll be there in a minute."

The minute was the longest of my life. By the time I got there, ambulances and fire trucks already swarmed the scene. Bystanders murmured and stared as I ran to where my husband's crumpled truck lay on its roof.

"Mom!" My daughter raced into my arms, a blur of golden hair and little arms and legs.

"Karen!" I screamed, wrapping my arms around her and raining kisses on her head. "Baby, I was so worried! I was so worried! I thought you were hurt!"

"I'm fine. But David and Randy …" I didn't hear the rest of what she said. I was racing, barreling toward them. Randy was on a stretcher in a neck brace, his leg sliced open. Firefighters crouched around the shattered car windows. The truck lay on its roof, workers milling around as sirens screamed. I rushed toward the car, and a woman stopped me, shielding me from the scene.

"I'm a nurse," she said. "Are you the mom?"

All I could do was nod dumbly.

"I just want you to know, there's angels everywhere." She led me closer to the truck, but all I could see was crumpled metal. My baby was trapped inside, and I couldn't even see him. "Talk to him," she urged, putting a hand on my shoulder. "Let him know you're here. Let him know the angels are here with him."

"David?" My voice was raspy, the words choking me. "David, it's okay. It's going to be okay. I love you, Mommy loves you."

As medical workers and firemen rushed around the truck, I kept talking, praying my words would soothe his pain, his fears. A fireman from our church walked up. I took one look into his eyes and I knew. Even before his lips moved, I knew.

My legs hit the ground, Dan's arms around me. All I remember was screaming.

かかか

Randy was airlifted to a local hospital to care for his wounds while we dealt with the logistics of David's death. The police were so kind as we numbly went through the motions, signing papers and giving statements. Karen stood next to me, watching the people around us. "They shouldn't keep staring," she muttered. "This isn't a show."

Before I could stop her, she calmly approached a man standing soberly at the edge of the crowd. It was the man who had caused the accident — a local principal who had been on his cell phone. His face was twisted with grief, shiny with tears and perspiration. He lifted his eyes to Karen, his lips trembling but silent.

She reached out and patted his arm gently. "We forgive you. And God forgives you," she said softly, sincerely.

Those words would not come so easily or so quickly for me.

The man burst into sobs at my daughter's gentle words, cradling his face in his hands. Karen returned to me. At just 14, she seemed to hold it together, with a strength I couldn't show her in my distress.

I turned to Dan, impatience gnawing at me. "We've got to get to my Randy," I whispered. "We've got to get to him."

❧❧❧

When you're in the middle of a tragedy, time slows down to minutes. It's everything you can do to get from one breath to another. I was devastated. After only eight years, my baby was gone. I had spent my life trying to shield my children from experiencing any of the troubles I went through in childhood. But David's death was the worst blow we had ever dealt with, and I couldn't protect any of us from it.

David's future was stolen from him — from us. We would never see him get his driver's license, go on a first date, attend his prom, graduate from college or marry and give us grandchildren. We would never see him become the wonderful husband and father we always knew he would be.

His life was one of the best gifts I'd ever been given. And now he was gone.

Still, I knew that he would want me to make the most of my own life. And to do that, I must determine to do what seemed impossible — forgive.

We held his funeral at our church, choosing to call it a celebration of life service instead. Part of the celebration included a call for people to find a second chance at life by believing in Jesus. David and I used to make lists of family and friends who we prayed for to know Jesus and ask for his forgiveness for their failures. I knew David would have been thrilled to see so many people checked off his list that day — including my own father.

Thinking about how much God had forgiven me for my own failures, I knew I had no right to be bitter toward the man who'd killed my son. A phrase David often spoke rang in my ears as if he was next to me.

"Everyone deserves a second chance," David would say.

Even the man who had snatched him away.

As a family, at church, we met with the man who caused the accident. We never pressed charges or threatened legal action, even though he willingly gave us his insurance information. A principal of a local school, we knew he was as tormented as we were. Even before he walked into the office, his pain radiated through the room. Clutching the hand of his wife, he stood, trembling.

"I know I can never replace David's life," he whispered. "I know I can't undo the damage that I caused." He raised his chin, tears streaming down his face. "But I pray that you can forgive me for the pain I caused you."

I looked at Dan, then back to this broken man. I extended my hand toward him, tears flooding my eyes. "David always believed everyone should get a second chance." I clutched his fingers, our tears falling between our feet. "I know he'd want you to have a second chance."

Breaking down in sobs, his fingers tightened around

mine as our pastor's voice wrapped around us like a warm comforter. "Dear Lord, let us pray …"

Still, I wondered if our family would get a second chance, too.

Dan and I tried for another baby. Not to replace David — no one could ever do that. But we were entering a new season as a family and wanted another child to be part of it.

Then, I miscarried. I desperately wanted another child, but after the miscarriage, I settled it in my heart that it wasn't meant to happen.

But I was about to get a second chance, too.

In January 2008, two years after David's death, I got a phone call from my sister. "Candis, you'll never believe it. The cousin of one of my co-workers is pregnant and doesn't want the baby. She can't keep it — she's already got three kids being taken care of by her mother. She's homeless and a drug addict and says she's just going to leave the baby at the hospital if someone doesn't want it. So," my sister finally paused for breath, "do you want it?"

My jaw dropped. Across the room, Dan stood, his eyebrows knit together. "She says there's a baby," I whispered. "No one wants her."

Dan opened his mouth, and the words running through my head fell from his lips. "We want her. Tell her we'll take her."

I held the phone up to my mouth. This time, my voice was strong and steady, confidence hammered into every word. "We want her. We want her."

A mere five days later, I rushed to the hospital after my phone rang, my sister calling to say Sally was in labor. I spent 12 hours with a woman I barely knew.

"I was going to get an abortion, you know." Sally stared up at me, daring me to judge her.

"I'm glad you didn't." I wrapped my fingers around hers. "This is very brave of you, giving up your daughter."

"It doesn't matter." Sally took a deep breath, gritting her teeth. "Just another mouth for my mom to feed. You'll be a better mother to her than I ever could."

"It doesn't have to be that way," I said, daring to push back fear and release my hope of a child if Sally would accept God's help and ours. Her fingers squeezed mine hard, her knuckles white. "You can change, Sally. God loves you so much. He will help you if you will trust him."

Even through the pain, bitterness twisted Sally's lips into a smile. "No one really loves me; I am not very loveable."

"But we can …" I fell silent as the nurse fluttered around, checking monitors and tubes.

"Okay, Sally. Push!" she cried. "Push!"

Sally's eyes met mine, and I nodded. "I'm here. I'm right here." Her fingers gripped tighter, nearly crushing my hand as a red-faced baby girl came screaming into the world.

"Take her away." Sally turned her head, closing her eyes. "Get her out of here! I don't want to see her!"

The baby was whisked to the NICU, and I was right behind her. This was the incredible moment where they banded us together with the little hospital bracelets stating mother and daughter. The nurse cleaned her up, wrapped her in a towel and placed her in my arms. I sucked in my breath, tears streaming down my face. My chest ached as my heart burst with more love than I'd ever felt in my life flooding every inch of my veins.

"I get it," I whispered, tears imprinting on my daughter's white towel. "I get it now." My mother and father always told me that they loved me as much as their birth children. They'd dedicated their lives to making me feel loved and accepted, but at times I had wondered if I really believed them.

"Candis? Dan is in the lobby." A nurse touched my shoulder.

"I'll go get him." Handing my new baby back to the nurse, I flew down the hall, nearly knocking Dan over as he jogged toward me. "She's here! She's perfect!"

"I knew she would be." Dan took my hand, and we hurried back to the hospital nursery where our new daughter was. Bursting through the doors with excitement, I stopped cold and sucked in my breath.

Sally was rocking the baby.

The bitterness I'd seen in her eyes during labor was now replaced with a look of wonder. Panic choked me, stealing my voice.

Dan and I just stared, myriad words stuck in our throats.

Sally looked up. A single tear streamed down her cheek as she shook her head. "I don't want you to think I changed my mind, I just had to say goodbye. She's not mine. She's yours."

Glancing down at this perfect little girl she had given birth to, love beamed from her smiling cheeks. "She deserves a home like yours. A family like yours." A second tear fell on the crumpled sheets, and the baby turned, a tiny warning cry piercing the air. "I just wanted to see her one last time."

She started to reach out to me with the baby, and I shook my head. I thought of our sweet David. "Take as much time as you need," I said. "We know how important it is to say goodbye."

"Are you sure?" She bit her lip and looked down. I followed Sally's gaze toward my daughter's tiny open eyes that looked up at me.

"She looks just like David." Dan's husky voice tickled my neck, his own tears dropping on my shoulders as he wrapped one arm around me, one arm around our new daughter. "Those perfect little features, that blond hair, just like an angel …"

"That smile." My voice wobbled as my lips curled up. "David always believed in second chances. A chance at forgiveness, a new start."

Sally's lips quivered, her smile slipping. "For the baby?"

"For everyone." I smiled at Sally. "So do we."

"Name?" The nurse poised over the birth certificate, pen ready.

"Tabitha," I whispered.

We knew then that she was God's reward for walking out tragedies with forgiveness, as David would. For forgiving, as Jesus did.

Through his death, David taught our family to forgive and to love again. Now Tabitha's life could only deepen that love and restore joy. There is still a big hole in our hearts from losing David, but thanks to God bringing Tabitha into our lives, our hearts have grown bigger so the hole seems a little smaller.

People often tell me how wonderful we are for taking in a baby who was destined for abortion or abandonment. I just look at them and smile.

"Everyone deserves a second chance," I tell them. "Everyone."

CONCLUSION

You do not have to walk in defeat, discouragement or confusion. God has a plan for your life ... a plan to prosper you, not to harm you, to give you hope and a future! (Jeremiah 29:11). He wants to empower you to overcome the trying obstacles that we regularly face. Every time we see another transformed and empowered life, it increases our awareness that God really loves people, and he is actively seeking to change lives. Think about it: How did you get this book? We believe you read this book because God brought it to you, seeking to reveal his love to you. Whether you're a man or a woman, a field worker or a waitress, blue collar or no collar, a parent or a student, we believe God came to save you. He came to save us. He came to save them. He came to save all of us from the hellish pain we've wallowed in and offer real joy and the opportunity to share in real life that will last forever through faith in Jesus Christ.

Do you have honest questions that such radical change is possible? It seems too good to be true, doesn't it? Each of us at Bethel Family Worship Center warmly invites you to come and check out our church family. Freely ask questions, examine our statements and see if we're for real. And, if you choose, journey with us at whatever pace you are comfortable. You will find that we are far from perfect. Our scars, and sometimes open wounds, are still healing, but we just want you to know God is still completing the process of authentic life change in us. We still make mistakes in our journey, like everyone will. Therefore, we acknowledge our continued need for each other's forgiveness and support because there are *No Easy Roads*. We need the love of God just as much as we did the day before we believed in him.

If you are unable to be with us, yet you intuitively sense you would really like to experience such a life change, here are some basic thoughts to consider. If you choose, at the end of this conclusion, you can pray the suggested prayer. If your prayer genuinely comes from your heart, you will experience the beginning stages of authentic life change, similar to those you have read about.

How does this change occur?

Recognize that what you're doing isn't working. Accept the fact that Jesus desires to forgive you for your bad decisions and selfish motives. Realize that without this forgiveness, you will continue a life separated from God and his amazing love. In the Bible, the book of Romans, chapter 6, verse 23 reads, "The reward for sin (seeking our way rather than God's way) is death, but the gift that God freely gives is everlasting life found in Jesus Christ" (God's Word Translation).

Believe in your heart that God passionately loves you and wants to give you a new heart. Ezekiel 11:19 reads, "I will give them singleness of heart and put a new spirit within them. I will take away their stony, stubborn heart and give them a tender, responsive heart" (New Living Translation).

Believe in your heart that "if you confess with your mouth that Jesus is Lord and believe in your heart that God raised him from the dead, you will be saved" (Romans 10:9, New Living Translation).

Believe in your heart that because Jesus paid for your failure and wrong motives, and because you asked him to forgive you, he has filled your new heart with his life in such a way that he transforms you from the inside out. Second Corinthians 5:17 reads, "This means that anyone who belongs to Christ has become a new person. The old life is gone; a new life has begun!" (NLT).

Why not pray now?

Lord Jesus, if I've learned one thing in my journey, it's that you are God and I am not. My choices have not resulted in the happiness I hoped they would bring. Not only have I experienced pain, I've also caused it. I know I am separated from you, but I want that to change. I am sorry for the choices I've made that have hurt myself, others and denied you. I believe your death paid for my sins, and you are now alive to change me from the inside out. Would you please do that now? I ask you to come and live in me so that I can sense you are here with me. Thank you for hearing and changing me. Now please help me know when you are talking to me, so I can cooperate with your efforts to change me. Amen.

Here in the Central Valley, the unfolding story of God's love is still being written … and your name is in it.

I hope to see you this Sunday!

Pastor Regan Sunderland
Bethel Family Worship Center
Tulare, California

We would love for you to join us at
Bethel Family Worship Center!

We meet Sunday mornings at 9 a.m. at
2516 North M Street, Tulare, CA 93274.

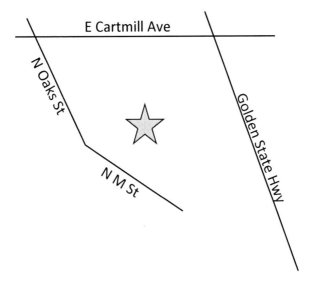

Please call us at 559.688.7545 for directions, or
contact us at www.tularebethel.org.

For more information on reaching your city with
stories from your church, please contact
Good Catch Publishing at
www.goodcatchpublishing.com

GOOD CATCH
PUBLISHING

Did one of these stories touch you?
Did one of these real people move you to tears?
Tell us (and them) about it on our reader blog at
www.goodcatchpublishing.blogspot.com.